W9-BNX-820

Main   Oct 2018

"Bravo, Anita! This book is a fun reference for anyone, whether they are a 'table for one' or a group of friends. As a professional chef, I too struggle with cooking for myself when I've spent the day cooking for everyone else, and I love that Anita has developed a guide. The playful anecdotes and stories of her solo escapades are enough for me to pick up this book, let alone the mouth-watering recipes that make me want to run to the kitchen to try them out. This is the perfect addition to your library!"

—APRIL BLOOMFIELD,
author of *A Girl and Her Pig*

"I learned to be a solo diner at Anita Lo's restaurant annisa. But even though I ate alone, I was never lonely, because her cooking spoke to my soul. This collection of recipes will dispel all forlorn thoughts about toiling over a hot stove by yourself. And it will give a celebratory new meaning to 'party of one.'"

—HOWARD CHUA-EOAN,
former news director of *Time*

This item no longer
belongs to Davenport
Public Library

ALSO BY ANITA LO

Cooking Without Borders
(with Charlotte Druckman)

SOLO

DAVENPORT PUBLIC LIBRARY
321 MAIN STREET
DAVENPORT, IOWA 52801

SOLO

A MODERN COOKBOOK FOR A PARTY OF ONE

ANITA LO

ILLUSTRATIONS BY JULIA ROTHMAN

ALFRED A. KNOPF  NEW YORK · 2018

THIS IS A BORZOI BOOK PUBLISHED BY ALFRED A. KNOPF

Copyright © 2018 by Anita Lo
Illustrations © 2018 by Julia Rothman

All rights reserved. Published in the United States by Alfred A. Knopf,
a division of Penguin Random House LLC, New York, and distributed in
Canada by Random House of Canada, a division of Penguin Random
House Canada Limited, Toronto.

www.aaknopf.com

Knopf, Borzoi Books, and the colophon are registered trademarks of
Penguin Random House LLC.

LIBRARY OF CONGRESS CATALOGING-IN-PUBLICATION DATA
Names: Lo, Anita, author. | Rothman, Julia, illustrator.
Title: Solo : a modern cookbook for a party of one / Anita Lo ;
illustrated by Julia Rothman.
Description: First edition. | New York : Alfred A. Knopf, 2018. |
Includes index.
Identifiers: LCCN 2017051096 (print) | LCCN 2017060204 (ebook) |
ISBN 9780451493606 (hardcover : alk. paper) |
ISBN 9780451493613 (ebook)
Subjects: LCSH: International cooking. | Cooking for one. |
LCGFT: Cookbooks.
Classification: LCC TX725.A1 .L5925 2018 (print) | LCC TX725.A1 (ebook) |
DDC 641.5/611—dc23
LC record available at https://lccn.loc.gov/2017051096

Cover illustrations by Julia Rothman
Cover design by Kelly Blair

Manufactured in China
First Edition

For Mary

CONTENTS

INTRODUCTION

I put the "Lo" in "solo." The A Lo in "alone." I've been dumped
almost as many times as I've been in relationships—and I
can count those on less than two hands. Spread over my fifty-
year life-span, that's a lot of solo meals. So if you consider
that—coupled with my many years working as a professional
chef—it seems that I'm particularly well suited to write
this book. Those chefs who say they can't cook for fewer
than forty people? Not me—I can do math. It is my Asian
birthright.

I'm also fanatical about waste. Waste is what makes
cooking for one, at least efficiently, so difficult. My parents
were Chinese, and my father survived the Cultural Revolution.
Food, at least at some point during their lives, was scarce;
as a result, I was taught never to waste one bit. In cooking
school at the Ritz Escoffier in Paris we were taught to utilize
every scrap, and at Bouley—my first cooking job—the sous
chef used to look through our garbage cans to make sure we
weren't being wasteful. It is an economic issue, but also an
ecological and social one. When I cook for myself, much of my
food involves using the often-overlooked but just-as-delicious
parts of meat and vegetables. For example, I grew up eating
broccoli stems as well as the florets. Instead of discarding
cabbage hearts, my mother gave them to me to snack on
raw while we were cooking. We didn't use radish leaves, but
they're virtually identical to turnip greens, so I generally cook
those along with the root itself, which helps you include

more dark green vegetables in your diet. And all those parts in the bag that comes inside of a chicken? If used properly, those parts are pure flavor—and another meal. Plus, cooking this way is important if you're working with fresh ingredients or on a budget.

The hospitalitarian in me also dictates that meals should be balanced. (Yeah, chefs are neurotic.) There must *always* be a vegetable or two. And your food should vary from day to day. It should be diverse in ingredients as well as in cultural provenance. Some days you'll want to eat light and healthy; on other days, butter is a perfectly good substitute for love. True hospitality extends to others and to yourself. Too often we forget about the latter. This book will help you to remember how to take care of yourself.

When I'm cooking at home, I generally make ingredient-focused dishes that are fast and easy—I leave the more complicated recipes for my professional life. I'll buy a whole chicken from a local, humane farmer, which might cost a little more, but I make sure that I use every bit. The first night I'll break it down and place the legs and wings in a vacuum sealer bag in usable portions to freeze. If I'm alone I'll do the same with one side of the breast, and cook the other for dinner. The bones and neck and gizzard will go into a stock right away or into the freezer for a later date. I'll either freeze the liver until I have enough to make a mousse or chopped liver, or I'll make a salad with it the next day, along with the heart, for a quick bistro lunch. Dining alone doesn't mean you're misanthropic. Nor does it have to be depressing. Cooking and dining alone can be one of the most blissful and empowering experiences you can have.

This book is for urban dwellers who would like to cook a fabulous, sophisticated meal for themselves, regardless of their circumstance. Although I have a soft spot for the depressed, jilted single, *Solo* is also for those who are happiest on their own, or those who are part of a fractured family, in whatever form—quite often these days, even if we're not single, we are left alone due to our partner's work/ family's social obligation. This book is also for those who have different tastes from their family or partner—why shouldn't they eat what they crave?

I hope you'll find that this book is the ultimate guide to self-love through the best means possible—delicious food— and that it helps you to celebrate your solitary moments. (If you happen to get a date, or just decide that you want to share, these recipes are easily multiplied by two.)

After all, they say the way to a person's heart is through the stomach. So far, it has worked for me.

. . . .•. •. •. . .. .• •••. •• .. •.. .•••

CHAPTER 1

VEGETABLE-FOCUSED MAINS

Roasted Stuffed Zucchini with Feta, Dill, and Cracked Wheat

The smell of dill can sometimes bring memories to mind of a strange day I spent in Greece. I adored Greece—I was awed by the history and architecture, inebriated by the sea-salt air, charmed by the people, and inspired by the food. But I did have one particularly harrowing, if comical, day while I was there. In 1997, my then-partner Jen and I took a year off to travel, and at some point decided it would be funny to make a pilgrimage to the island of Lesvos, and, in particular, to Sappho's birthplace, Skala Eressos. Aside from the obvious gay attraction, we were lured by our guidebook's promises of a spiritual community, sandy beaches, great restaurants, and a lovely trip through olive groves on the way there.

The day started out in Mitilini, where we boarded the first of two buses to take us across the island to our destination. We were early, so we took our seats by the back door. The bus was empty save the two of us, and we were beginning to think that Eressos wasn't a particularly popular destination. Then, just as the bus was about to depart, a horde of about twenty-five older women, all wearing black dresses, some mustachioed and missing teeth, and none taller than five feet, came out of the corner of the parking lot, rushing the bus en masse. I was momentarily terrified, and I heard Jen squeak pitifully as the first wave pushed their way onto the bus. This clearly wasn't the gay pride experience I had in mind! Things settled down after that, and we got to our first stop unscathed, at least physically, and chuckling about the experience.

The next bus, by contrast, was filled with only younger men, all locals who gave us disapproving, knowing looks as we boarded. It was an old, rickety school bus, and we took our seats at the very back to stay out of the way. The view as we climbed the olive tree–dotted hills was gorgeous, but the route was steep and endlessly winding. The old bus seemed about to tip over at any moment, from one side to the other. Luckily, we had an empty bag that had once held *koulouri* (a bagel-like bread topped with sesame seeds); I've never felt so sick in my life. But this is a cookbook, so I won't go into it further.

Once we arrived, we found a small bed-and-breakfast right on the beach owned by a Lesvian lesbian couple. At last, we had found our spiritual community! Then, as we exited the hotel in search of dinner, we came upon the owners screaming at each other. The next day, when we went down to breakfast, there was no one to be found. So much for that.

This recipe is taken from a staff meal I later prepared that was inspired by that trip to Greece. As they say, when life gives you lemons, make *avgolemeno* (or something like that).

· Cut off the stem of the zucchini, then cut in half lengthwise. Using a spoon, scrape the inner, softer, seeded area onto a cutting board and then slice it. Don't worry too much about slicing this perfectly—it won't matter in the end. Preheat your oven or toaster oven to 375°F.

· Place bulgur in a small bowl, cover with ⅓ cup boiling water and a pinch of salt, then cover with plastic wrap and allow to steep for at least 5 minutes, while you prepare the stuffing.

· In a small skillet, heat 2 tablespoons of the olive oil on medium and add the onions. Sweat them (get them hot and have them release their liquid without browning) until they are soft and translucent, then add the garlic and the sliced inner part of the zucchini. Season with salt and pepper and stir until gently cooked.

· In a small bowl, beat the egg, then add the cooked ingredients, plus the feta, herbs, currants, 1 teaspoon of the lemon juice, and lemon zest. Lightly season to taste with salt and pepper. Use the remaining tablespoon of oil to coat the zucchini boats, then season both sides with salt and pepper. Stuff the cavities with the feta mixture and then bake the boats on a small tray until cooked through, about 15–20 minutes.

· Uncover the steeped bulgur and fluff with a fork. Stir in the remaining lemon juice and 1 tablespoon of olive oil.

· Serve zucchini on top of a bed of bulgur.

1 medium zucchini, about 8 inches long

¼ cup medium-grain bulgur

3 tablespoons olive oil

½ small onion or 1 slice of a larger one, diced (about ¼ cup)

½ clove garlic, finely chopped

1 egg

¼ cup crumbled feta cheese

2 tablespoons chopped dill or mint or both

1 heaping teaspoon currants (optional)

2 teaspoons lemon juice

A few grates of lemon zest, using a microplane grater

Salt and black pepper to taste

Avocado and Sunchoke Ochazuke

· · · · · · · ·• · •·· · · · ·· · · · ·• •· · · •·· · · · ·•·

The Japanese word *ochazuke* comes from *O*, which is an honorific, *cha*, meaning "tea," and *tsuke*, meaning "submerged." It is often eaten as a quick snack or a way to use up old rice, and thus is a perfect dish when cooking for one. If you cook and eat rice often, I'd suggest making larger batches and reheating it either in the microwave or in a steamer to save on steps. My mother used to always add any leftover plain rice back into the new pot at the end of its cooking so that nothing would ever go to waste.

This is a very versatile recipe—you can change it or add toppings to your liking; it is also a good way to use up any bits of leftover plain fish, meat, or vegetables. Substitute brown rice for a nuttier, more nutritious meal, or spice it up with some *togarashi* (Japanese chili) or *furikake* (rice seasoning).

NOTE

This dish is also quite nice when topped with a fried or poached egg, or a bit of cooked fish. When plated, it should be mostly rice with a puddle of dashi/tea broth that is scooped up to flavor the rice.

· Toss the sunchoke slices with the oil and season with salt and pepper. Place on a tray in the toaster oven and toast on dark, or brown in a little oil in a small sauté pan.

· Heat the dashi and let steep with the green tea for 3 minutes, then strain. Add the soy sauce and mirin and stir (this may seem a little too salty, but it needs to season the plain rice and avocado). Top the rice with the toasted sunchokes, then with the sliced avocado and sliced kombu, then with the scallions, nori, toasted sesame seeds, and the simmered bonito mixture, if using. Just before eating, pour the hot dashi over the top.

Two 2-inch pieces sunchoke, sliced about ¼ inch thick

2 teaspoons oil

Salt and black pepper to taste

1 cup dashi (see recipe page 172)

1 teaspoon green tea (or 1 tea bag, optional)

3 tablespoons soy sauce

1 tablespoon plus 2 teaspoons mirin

1 cup cooked short-grain white or brown rice

½ ripe Hass avocado, sliced

1 small square kombu, about 4 x 4 inches, rinsed, left over from dashi recipe, and dried

1 tablespoon scallion greens, cut on a bias

1 large pinch shredded or torn nori

1 large pinch toasted sesame seeds (they can be bought this way in Asian markets, or you can toast them yourself in a dry pan on high heat, stirring constantly—do a larger batch and keep in an airtight container)

1 tablespoon simmered bonito (optional, see Don't Waste It, page 172)

Twice-Cooked Sweet Potatoes with Kale, Mushrooms, and Parmesan

. . . .

At annisa, we always try to have an appetizer on the menu that would be suitable as a vegetarian main course. In order for it to be placed on our menu, I require that this option appeal to the omnivore as well. This dish is based on a Roman gnocco (a ricotta-based dumpling) that we once served with kabocha squash, maitake mushrooms, lacinato kale, and Podda Classico cheese. It delivers the same earthy, sweet flavors, punctuated by the umami of the cheese and made complex with herbs. Only it takes a tenth of the time to make.

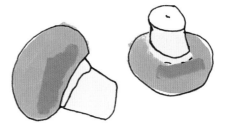

- Prick the sweet potato with a fork all over, then place on a plate and microwave on high until a knife easily pierces the thickest part, about 8–10 minutes. Preheat your toaster or regular oven to 350°F. Cut the sweet potato in half, then scoop out most of the interior into a bowl and mash with the ricotta or mascarpone, and a healthy grating (about a tablespoon) of Parmesan. Season to taste with salt and pepper. This potato mixture does not need to be completely smooth. Stuff it back into the potato skins, then bake, drizzled with a little olive oil, until lightly browned on top, about 15 minutes.

- In the meantime, prepare the mushrooms and kale. Heat a skillet on high, then add the 3 tablespoons of olive oil. Add the mushroom slices in one layer and let cook for a minute until starting to brown. Then add the kale, garlic, and salt and pepper, and stir until wilted and lightly browned. Add the thyme, then stir once again.

- When the sweet potatoes are ready, top with the mushroom-kale mixture. Finish with more grated Parmesan and eat.

1 sweet potato or yam

3 tablespoons fresh ricotta or mascarpone cheese

1 tablespoon grated Parmesan cheese, plus extra for serving

Salt and black pepper to taste

3 tablespoons olive oil, plus extra for drizzling

4–5 cremini mushrooms (or any fresh mushroom will do), fairly thickly sliced (about 1/3 inch)

Handful of washed kale (any kind—you can use the salad greens that come prewashed to save time, see Kale Salad with Dates and Tahini Dressing, page 158)

1/2 clove garlic, finely chopped

A pinch of fresh thyme leaves (substitute half that amount if using dried—a mini pinch)

Shaved Root Vegetable Salad with Smoked Salmon, Capers, and an Egg

. . . .

would never eat just a salad for dinner. My inner chubby child would have a breakdown. But I understand that many of you are perfectly content with such lighter fare. Here's an easy, composed salad that I would have for a weekend lunch, or perhaps after dinner service at the restaurant when we've had a substantial staff meal at 4:30 in the afternoon. Round it out with some Crushed Baby Potatoes (see recipe page 149) or a Steamed Artichoke with Lemon and Herb Butter (page 154)—or better still, if you're just like me, a well-marbled, thick steak.

. . . .

1 large handful (or about 2 cups loosely packed) thinly shaved mixed root vegetables such as carrots, radishes, celery root, baby turnips, and candy cane beets (use a Japanese mandolin or, if necessary, a peeler)

2 slices smoked salmon, cut into strips (about 1¾–2 ounces)

½ tablespoon drained capers

3 slices red onion

1 tablespoon chopped dill or chives (optional)

1 teaspoon Dijon mustard

1 teaspoon lemon juice

2 tablespoons olive oil

Salt and black pepper to taste

1 egg

. . . .

· Place shaved vegetables, salmon, capers, onions, herbs if using, mustard, lemon juice, and 1 tablespoon of the olive oil with the salt and pepper in a bowl and mix. Taste and adjust seasonings if necessary.

· Heat a nonstick sauté pan on high, and add the second tablespoon of olive oil. Crack the egg into the pan, season with salt and pepper, and fry to desired consistency. Mound salad onto a plate and top with the hot egg, seasoning again with salt and pepper. Eat with some crusty bread and butter.

Cauliflower Chaat with Almonds

I n September 2015, I traveled through northern India—alone, of course. To be fair, I was brought there by a wonderful charity called Creative Services Support Group to help raise funds. The organization takes homeless girls off the streets, teaches them to cook, and then helps them find jobs in the hospitality industry. I was there, along with several other female chefs from around the world, cooking for a series of gala fundraisers and teaching classes to the girls. When that was over, I was supposed to travel for five days with my good friend April Bloomfield, who unfortunately had to drop out at the last minute due to an impending restaurant opening. (Dumped again, and we weren't even going out!)

The organizers of the events were so worried that we would get "Delhi belly" that over the two weeks I was cooking there, they had us eating only in high-end, Westernized restaurants or in our very fancy hotels. By the end, I was worried that I would never see the other part of India. Luckily, Akriti, a cook who had trained with me at annisa and whom I had (unsuccessfully) tried to hire, noticed that I was going to be in her hometown. I organized for her to cook with me at my second gala. Then on my last day in Delhi, she and her brother took me around town to try all kinds of everyday Indian treats, including street food. This recipe is inspired by some of the delicious food we had that day. The word *chaat* means "snack," but this dish is rich and complex enough to serve as a vegetarian main course.

Akriti came with me to Jaipur, just north of Delhi, so I wasn't entirely alone on this most amazing trip. And I never once got sick.

• Heat the oil in a sauté pan on high until the oil just starts to smoke in small wisps. Add the cauliflower florets, then lower the heat to medium high. Sprinkle with salt and allow to brown, then stir and turn heat down further to medium. Cook for 1 minute more, then add the ginger and jalapeño and stir. Add the chopped cilantro, lemon juice, and *chaat masala* and stir again. Remove from the heat and allow to sit while you make your sauce.

• Place all the sauce ingredients in the container that came with your hand blender, or a container with a similar depth and small circumference so the blades will be submerged when you blend your sauce. Puree until smooth, repositioning the blades every so often to get all the cilantro incorporated. Taste and adjust salt and pepper.

• Toast the almonds in a toaster oven or a regular oven preheated to 375°F until browned and fragrant. If your almonds are pre-roasted, skip this step.

• Drizzle the sauce over the cauliflower, strew the almonds on top, and serve with some cooked rice or store-bought naan.

Don't Waste It!

See recipe on page 167 for what to do with leftover cauliflower.

FOR THE CAULIFLOWER

3 tablespoons vegetable oil, or other non-flavored oil such as canola

½ small head cauliflower, cut into large florets

Salt to taste

2 teaspoons finely chopped ginger

2 teaspoons finely chopped jalapeño, or to taste

1 tablespoon chopped cilantro

½ teaspoon lemon juice

2 teaspoons *chaat masala*

FOR THE SAUCE

1 cup cilantro, loosely packed

1 teaspoon finely chopped jalapeño

1 heaping tablespoon finely chopped onion

½ small clove garlic

2 tablespoons plain full-fat Greek yogurt

2 tablespoons water

A pinch of cumin

A pinch of *chaat masala*

1 teaspoon lemon juice

Salt and pepper to taste

TO SERVE

1 heaping tablespoon roughly chopped almonds

Smoky Eggplant and Scallion Frittata

. . . .·· ·.. . . . .·· ··. . . .. . .·· ·

Here's a tongue twister: *Tortang Talong in Tagolog*. Say that three times fast! My sister's Filipina nanny Evelyn made this dish for me one day when I was visiting them in Hong Kong. I'm pretty sure I only had it that one time, but it was crave-worthy and memorable. It took her less than thirty minutes to make, and is thus perfect for a dinner at home alone. Pair it with some Stir-Fried Greens with Garlic (page 152), and you have a well-balanced meal to eat that's easy on the palate (if not the tongue).

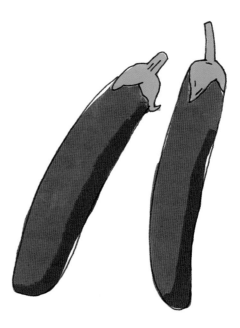

- Fire-roast the whole eggplant by turning your gas burner on high and placing the eggplant directly in the flames.

- When blackened (after about 3 minutes or so), turn using a pair of tongs and repeat on the remaining sides. Allow to cool, then peel off the blackened skin and season both sides with salt and pepper. (If you don't have a gas burner, you can broil the eggplant in the oven as close as possible to the heat source, until it is blackened on all sides. This won't give you the same smoky intensity, but it will do.)

- Place a nonstick skillet large enough to hold the eggplant over high heat. Add the oil, and when it is just smoking, add the ground pork or beef, if using, and break up with a spoon.

- Season with salt and pepper and stir. Add the garlic and the scallion whites and stir again. The meat should be cooked through at this point. Beat the eggs with the oyster sauce and the scallion greens. Lower the heat to medium, add the eggs, and stir. Immediately add the eggplant—with the stem side just sticking out to one side—and mash the body into the egg mixture. Fold the sides of the omelet up and over the eggplant, then flip and cook through. Serve with the rice.

1 Japanese or baby eggplant

Salt and black pepper to taste

3 tablespoons vegetable or other non-flavored oil such as canola

¼ pound ground pork or beef (optional)

½ garlic clove, finely chopped

1 scallion, sliced on a bias, whites and green parts separated

2 eggs

1 tablespoon oyster sauce

1 cup cooked rice

Roasted and Pickled Radish Tacos

.............•..............•.....••.....•.

'm not one of those old, French-trained chefs who turn up their noses at vegetarians. Really! Some of my best friends are vegetarians. Case in point: I have a good friend, Amanda Cohen of Dirt Candy, who makes the most amazing brussels sprout tacos, to which these owe their conception. Her tacos are much more elaborate, with various sauces and condiments, and you must go try them. These are much simpler and are easy and inexpensive to produce on a weeknight. Either are healthy alternatives to the usual meat ones … whether you're one of those people or not. (Just kidding!)

· Preheat a toaster oven or oven to 400°F. Place the majority of the radishes, their tops, the olive oil, the tomatillo, and half the jalapeño in a bowl, season with salt and pepper, and toss. Remove the tomatillo and jalapeño and place to one side of the roasting pan. Add the cumin and cinnamon to the bowl with the radishes and toss again. Remove the radishes and place to the other side of the roasting pan. Bake until everything is softened, about 12–15 minutes.

· In the meantime, make the radish pickles: Cut the remaining 3 radishes into thin rounds and place in a small ramekin or bowl along with the onions, the other half of the jalapeño, and the smashed garlic. In a small sauté pan, bring the vinegar and three tablespoons water to a boil, then pour over the sliced radish mixture. Set aside to cool to room temperature.

· When the roasting vegetables are soft, remove the tomatillo and jalapeño and place them in the container that came with your immersion blender. Add the radish greens to the baking pan and replace in the oven. Cook until wilted and remove. Taste and adjust salt and pepper. Place the remaining third of the garlic clove in with the tomatillo and the sprig of cilantro, the teaspoon of lime juice, and the water, and blend with the hand blender, to make a smooth salsa. Season to taste with salt and pepper.

· Reheat the tortillas in a dry hot sauté pan, or on top of the toaster oven, one by one. Make the tacos with the roasted radishes, garnished with a little salsa, pickles, and queso fresco. (Serve with wedges of lime if desired.)

1 bunch radishes with tops intact, washed (reserve the tops and the 3 smallest radishes for later; quarter the rest)

2 tablespoons olive oil

One 2-inch tomatillo, husk removed, cut in half

1 small jalapeño, stem removed, cut lengthwise (or to taste: jalapeños vary greatly on the Scoville scale, so keep that in mind when using)

Salt and black pepper to taste

1 large pinch cumin

1 small pinch cinnamon

One 1/3-inch slice medium onion

1 clove garlic (smash 2/3, set aside remaining 1/3)

2 tablespoons white vinegar or cider vinegar

5 tablespoons water

1 sprig cilantro

1 teaspoon lime juice

TO SERVE

4 small corn tortillas

1/4 cup queso fresco, crumbled

Wedge of lime (optional— there should be enough acidity from the pickles and salsa)

A Single, Broken Egg on a Bed of Torn, Wilted, Bitter Greens with Blue Cheese

. . . .·. . . . .·. . . . .·. . .

've always used Valentine's Day as an excuse to set free my corny, cloyingly sappy, and sick inner child. I blame Hallmark (and, like everyone else, my mother). My first Valentine's Day menu when I was the chef at Maxim's was full of the requisite and obvious red and pink ingredients, heart-shaped cutouts and hearts of foods, passion fruit and edible flowers, but I always set aside at least one dish for the jilted lover. I think my first one had something to do with monkfish and extra-virgin olive oil, and it has been a long downward spiral ever since.

· Place the greens, cheese, prunes, and herbs in bowl. In a small nonstick sauté pan, melt the butter over high heat and add the mixture. Cook until everything is beginning to brown (or blacken—so you can have black and blue in the recipe as well!), then remove from heat and add the shallot and the hazelnuts, and stir. Add the red wine vinegar and pour over the greens. Season with salt and pepper and toss it all together. Wipe the sauté pan clean and add the olive oil.

· Place on medium-high heat and cook the egg sunny-side up, or as you like it. Season once again with salt and pepper, and top the salad with the egg. Eat me.

2 ounces bitter greens, such as escarole, endive, or mustard greens, washed and torn into bite-size pieces

1½ ounces blue cheese, crumbled

3 prunes, roughly chopped

Pinch of chopped herbs such as chives, tarragon, thyme, or parsley (or a mixture)

2 tablespoons butter

1 teaspoon shallot, minced

8 hazelnuts, crushed

2 teaspoons red wine vinegar

Salt and black pepper to taste

1 tablespoon olive oil

1 egg

A healthy dose of self-pity

Broccoli Rabe Pesto and Charred Orange Toast

This is a good way to use up leftover broccoli rabe. The pesto can be frozen for later use—just place in a sealed container with a thin layer of oil on the top to prevent freezer burn if you can't use it all. And you can substitute another bitter green if desired. Or substitute the bread for some cooked pasta. Recipe creation is iterative. Feel free to experiment.

. . . . .

⅓ bunch broccoli rabe, bottoms cut off and cleaned

¼ cup olive oil, plus 1 tablespoon

1 clove garlic

3 tablespoons grated Parmesan cheese

Salt and black pepper to taste

½ clementine, peeled and separated into segments

1–2 pieces thickly cut, crusty bread

A couple of shavings of Parmesan cheese (use a peeler)

A drizzle of finishing olive oil (optional)

1 Calabrian chili (optional)

· Bring a large pot of water to a boil and season amply with salt so that it tastes like seawater. Add the broccoli rabe and cook until tender (about 3–4 minutes), drain, run under cold water, and squeeze dry. Roughly chop and add it to the bowl of a food processor, along with ¼ cup of the olive oil and the garlic. Puree, then add Parmesan, and season to taste with salt and pepper.

· Heat a small sauté pan on high for a good 2 minutes.

· Add the tablespoon of olive oil, and, when smoking, add the clementines. Season with salt and pepper, then char the clementines on both sides. Remove from the heat. Toast the bread and top with a thick layer of the broccoli rabe pesto, then the orange and the shaved Parmesan. Drizzle with a little finishing olive oil and a few dots of Calabrian chili, if desired. Eat by itself, or with a roasted Italian sausage.

CHAPTER 2

NOODLES AND RICE

Beef and Kimchee Noodle Soup

··········•··•··············•··········••·

Growing up in suburban Michigan, I always wanted to distance myself from my Asian heritage. After all, I felt like it wasn't really my culture—I was raised in a white neighborhood with a live-in Hungarian nanny and an Anglo-Saxon stepfather. But I came back to it through cooking food: first at a Vietnamese restaurant in Soho, then at a Korean-owned restaurant on Fifth Avenue, whose owners sent me to cooking school in Seoul for a week before opening. Of course, I'm Chinese, not Vietnamese or Korean—but too often, Americans tend to lump all the multiple nationalities of eastern Asia into one, so work with me here. I still sometimes feel rebellious pangs when I get one too many requests to speak about Chinese food or cook something Asian, as I trained in France and worked at both Bouley and Chanterelle. But one of the many times in my adulthood when I felt at home in my Chinese identity was while watching the animated film *Kung Fu Panda*.

There's a point in the movie where Mr. Ping, a noodle soup chef who happens to be a duck, says to his son, the protagonist Po the Panda, "We are noodle folk. Broth runs through our veins!" In that hilarious moment, I found my soul.

FOR THE SHORT RIB

14 ounces short rib, defatted
and bone in, cut into 2 pieces:
one approximately twice the
size of the other, leaving the
bone attached to both at
the bottom

Salt and black pepper

2 tablespoons vegetable oil or
other non-flavored oil such as
canola

½ small onion, sliced (about
⅔ cup)

1 quart chicken stock

1 clove garlic, smashed

. . . .·.•·•·.....·..··.•.··....·.•• ••·•··•...• •·•

· Braise the short rib (skip this section if using already-
braised meat and stock): Season both short rib pieces with
salt and pepper on all sides. Heat a sauté pan on high.
(If you're not using an electric slow cooker for the soup,
you can use a medium pot here instead.) Add the oil to
the pan and swirl, and when it's smoking, add the meat.
Lower heat to medium high and brown meat on all sides.
Remove meat, add the onions to the pan, and reduce heat
to medium. Cook, stirring occasionally, until onions are soft
and translucent, about 4 minutes. If using a pot, place meat
back inside with any juices that have accumulated, cover
with chicken stock, and add the garlic. Bring to a boil and
skim, then turn to a simmer and cook, 3–3½ hours after the
boil, adding additional stock or water as necessary to keep
the short rib submerged. If using an electric slow cooker,
place meat, juices, onions, garlic, and stock in the cooker,
cover, set to low, and leave for 8–10 hours. Skim the top of
fat, and remove the smaller piece of meat, discarding the
bone. Reserve 2 cups of the broth.

· **FOR THE SOUP:** Heat a small pot on medium high. Add the oils, then the onions, and cook, stirring, until onions are translucent. Add the garlic and ground chili and stir, then add the kimchee and stir again. Rinse the kombu and add along with the dried anchovies and cover with the 2 reserved cups broth. Bring to a boil, skim, then simmer while you cut the carrots, shred the meat, and cook the noodles. When the kombu is reconstituted, remove and cut into bite-size strips and replace in the pot.

· Cook the noodles in salted water per the instructions on the package. Season the broth with the soy sauce, fish sauce, and sugar, and add the carrots and shredded beef. Cook until carrots are just cooked, retaining some texture, about 1 minute. Drain noodles and place in a bowl. Top with the beef and broth, then garnish with the scallions.

Don't Waste It!

See recipe on page 144 for what to do with leftover short rib.

FOR THE SOUP

1 tablespoon vegetable oil or other non-flavored oil such as canola

1 teaspoon sesame oil

1 slice onion, halved

½ clove garlic, finely chopped

1 teaspoon Korean ground chili (optional)

⅓ cup kimchee with juices

1 small piece kombu (about 2 x 4 inches)

1 tablespoon dried anchovies (iriko)

2 cups broth, defatted from above (see method)

¼ cup carrots, julienned

⅓ of the short rib from above, shredded

TO SERVE

2½ ounces dry udon noodles or 4 ounces fresh, cooked per package instructions (use salted water)

1 tablespoon soy sauce

1 tablespoon fish sauce

1 teaspoon sugar

1 tablespoon scallion greens, cut on the bias

Chicken Pho

The sight of plastic children's furniture—squat tables and wee stools in bright colors—always makes me think of pho. When I visited Vietnam fifteen years ago, this was often the way pho was served: at mini outdoor, portable restaurants with makeshift stoves and full-size customers crouched over steaming bowls of noodle soup. For something like 50 cents you got a big bowl, light and bright with lime and herbs, yet filling and well rounded as a meal. It is served at all times of the day, but it remains one of my favorite breakfast foods. Here is a chicken version that will cost you a little more than 50 cents to make, but you'll get to eat it on more comfortable, adult-size furniture.

- In a small pot (about a 2-quart pot) heat the oil on low. Add the shallot and stir. Cook, stirring occasionally, until golden brown throughout, then remove the majority to a clean paper towel and season with salt and pepper. Drain excess oil from the pot (leaving the remaining portion of browned shallots).

- Season the chicken with salt and pepper and add to the pot along with the ginger, garlic, scallion white, and cilantro stem (and lemongrass, if using) and cover with cold water. Place on high heat and bring to a boil. Skim, turn to a simmer, and cook 20 minutes or until cooked through. Remove chicken to a plate and strain remaining stock. You should have about 2 cups of broth left; if not, add water to make 2 cups. Season broth with fish sauce.

- Cook the noodles per the package instructions (you'll need to salt the water regardless of what they say) and drain. Shred the chicken thigh and leg meat and discard the bones. You can shred the chicken wing meat or leave it to eat whole. Place drained noodles in the bowl with the seasoned broth, then top with the chicken meat, the scallion greens, and the browned shallots. Serve with the beansprouts, herbs, jalapeño, lime, and chili sauce on the side (if using).

2 tablespoons oil

1 small shallot, thinly sliced

Salt and black pepper to taste

1 skinless chicken leg, thigh, and wing

One 1/8-inch (approx.) slice ginger

1 clove garlic, smashed

1 scallion white, halved lengthwise

1 cilantro stem (save leaves for garnish)

One 5-inch piece lemongrass pounded with a meat hammer or small saute pan to crush and release its oils (optional)

2 tablespoons fish sauce (or to taste)

2½ ounces dry rice vermicelli

1 teaspoon scallion greens, chopped

½ cup fresh beansprouts

3 large leaves Thai basil

3 large leaves mint

3 thin slices jalapeño (optional)

1 wedge lime

Tuong Ot Toi Vietnam chili-garlic sauce (optional)

Spaghetti with Burst Baby Tomatoes and Chili

....

Jarred Calabrian chilies changed my life. Okay, maybe that is a slight exaggeration, but food *is* my life, and adding them to my arsenal of ingredients has expanded my culinary horizons . . . so yes, the peppers have certainly had an effect on my existence in a delightfully piquant way. Rich with olive oil and slightly acidic from fermentation, the condiment adds a soulful, savory base that wakes up the palate as well as the other ingredients. I'd had them in dishes before my friend Elizabeth Falkner brought some out to my house on Long Island, but had never tasted them by themselves until then. She made a handmade pasta with the chilies, along with capers, currants, olives, anchovies, and pine nuts, which bowled me over. Ever since, I've been using them in stews, on pizza, with fish and shellfish, and even with rabbit on the menu at annisa. Here is an easy, everyday dish made exciting with the addition of this transformative pepper.

· Bring a pot of water to a boil and season amply with salt (it should taste like seawater). Add the spaghetti and stir. Cook until al dente (follow the directions on the package).

· In the meantime, heat a 10-inch sauté pan on high and add the olive oil. Add the garlic and swirl, then add the tomatoes and the wine or water. Turn to a simmer and cook for about 8 minutes. The tomatoes should burst (you can press on the few that don't with a spatula to help them along) and create a thickened, chunky sauce. Season with salt and pepper, and add the Calabrian chili.

· When the pasta is done, remove from the water with tongs or a strainer and add to the sauté pan. Cook briefly, stirring, then stir in 2 tablespoons of the Parmesan. Taste and adjust seasonings. Place in a bowl, tear the basil over the top, and garnish with the remaining Parmesan.

3 ounces spaghetti

2 tablespoons olive oil

½ clove garlic, finely chopped

1 cup ripe cherry tomatoes

¼ cup white wine or water

Salt and black pepper to taste

1 teaspoon crushed Calabrian chili condiment

3 tablespoons grated Parmesan cheese

3 leaves basil

Gnocchi with Mortadella, Peas, and Pistachios

························

Tourists flock to Tuscany and Sicily and the cities of Venice and Rome for good reason, but if you are a true food nerd, as I am, you haven't really experienced Italy until you've been to Emilia-Romagna. Emilia-Romagna is the breadbasket of Italy. It is where much of the best, most well-known Italian ingredients are produced—Parmigiano Reggiano, Balsamico di Modena, and Prosciutto di Parma all hail from the region. Tartufi bianchi di Alba? Baloney! Most of the country's white truffles come from Savigno, another quaint town in that region. . . . Which brings me to real baloney, or Mortadella di Bologna, a giant smooth sausage flavored with myrtle berries and speckled with cubes of fat. When I visited Bologna, I happened upon a mortadella festival in the center of town and fell in love tasting all the subtle differences between the mortadella from the various producers in the region, of which there were dozens. Best of all, there was a woman dressed entirely in pink mortadella print from her hat to her gown to her shoes.

- Make the gnocchi (or substitute store-bought and skip this section): Prick the potato all over with a fork and microwave on high for about 8–10 minutes or until a knife inserted into the thickest portion goes in easily. Cut in half, scoop out the flesh, and, while it's hot, pass through a ricer or pound through a metal cone strainer, or press through a wire mesh strainer using a rubber spatula. (Use the plastic feeder tool if you have one from a food processor or a blender with the cone strainer; if using a wire mesh strainer, find one that isn't too fine or it will be more difficult to push the potato through). Season the mound of potato with salt and pepper and dust with the flour. Flatten the mound gently and drizzle a little of the beaten egg (about a tablespoon) over the top and mix. Add more egg if necessary, just to bring the mixture together in a dough that can be formed into logs. Knead lightly until ingredients are evenly dispersed. Roll, dusting lightly with more flour to prevent sticking, into tubes about ⅓ inch in diameter. Don't try to make just one big tube; several tubes will be easier to handle. Cut tubes into ¾-inch lengths.

- Bring a pot of water to a boil and season amply with salt (it should taste like seawater). Heat a 10-inch sauté pan on high, add the olive oil, then the garlic and the mortadella, and stir. When sizzling, add ¼ cup of the boiling water, then add the butter and swirl to incorporate while boiling. Add the peas and pistachios and remove from the heat. Add the gnocchi to the pot of boiling water and gently stir.

- When the gnocchi are floating, remove with a slotted spoon or skimmer and place in the sauté pan with the other ingredients, along with the Parmesan and the remaining egg. Stir and season to taste with salt, pepper, and lemon juice and zest. Stir, then plate and top with more Parmesan.

FOR THE GNOCCHI

1 Idaho potato (about 10 ounces)

Salt and black pepper

¼ cup flour

1 egg, beaten with a pinch of salt

FOR THE MORTADELLA, PEAS, AND PISTACHIOS

2 tablespoons olive oil

½ small clove garlic, finely chopped

2 ounces mortadella, cut into strips (1 inch long by ¼ inch wide)

2 tablespoons butter

¼ cup peas (just-picked and shelled English peas are ideal, but frozen petite peas make a fine, easily obtainable substitute)

2 tablespoons roughly chopped shelled pistachios

TO SERVE

2 tablespoons Parmesan cheese, plus more for topping

Salt and black pepper to taste

½ teaspoon lemon juice, or to taste

A few gratings of lemon zest on a microplane

Fresh Pasta with Anchovies, Charred Lemons, and Radish

You really don't have to make your own pasta, but I can't stress enough how easy it is. And it's a great thing to cook when you just want to make dinner from whatever you have lying around. Nothing beats that fresh pasta bite, nor the satisfaction that comes from making something from scratch. This is a lesson in how little it takes to put together a tasty meal from your basic pantry.

. . . . .

FOR THE PASTA (OR SUBSTITUTE STORE-BOUGHT FRESH OR DRY TAGLIATELLE OR LINGUINE)

100 grams flour (about 1 cup)

1 egg

1 teaspoon olive oil

1 pinch salt

· **MAKE THE PASTA:** Place the flour on a clean surface or cutting board and make a well in the center about 3 inches in diameter. Add the egg, the olive oil, and the salt to the well and beat with a fork. When egg is beaten, start bringing in some of the walls of the well, leaving the outer wall intact. When the center is pasty, you can use a spatula or bench scraper to fold the flour over the top, cutting in the flour so it incorporates into the egg mixture. Use your hands to knead the rest into a ball of dough. If the flour won't fully incorporate after a good 2 minutes of hand mixing, add a little water to bring it all together. Knead until smooth and elastic, about 6 minutes, then cover with plastic wrap and allow to rest 20–30 minutes. The dough should not stick to your hands or the work surface, but should be bouncy and pliable. If it is sticky, add a tablespoon of flour and knead again until it is the right consistency. Once the dough is rested, roll as thin as possible using a rolling pin (about 1/16 inch thick) or use a pasta machine until the pasta is somewhat translucent. Dust as necessary with flour to keep dough from sticking. Allow to dry a little, then roll and cut into thin, even strips about 1/4 inch thick.

· Bring a pot of water to a boil and generously salt it. Heat a 10-inch sauté pan on high for 1–2 minutes. Add the 2 tablespoons of olive oil and when just smoking, add the lemon triangles in a single layer and sear until browned. Turn heat down to medium high, turn the lemons, and add the anchovies, garlic, and radish slices and greens if using, and stir. Blanch the pasta in the boiling water, stirring just after you add it. Cook for 2 minutes, then remove to the sauté pan using tongs or a strainer. Add the 2 tablespoons of grated Parmesan and toss. Season with salt and pepper, if necessary, to taste. Place in a shallow bowl and top with a little finishing olive oil and more Parmesan if desired.

FOR THE ANCHOVIES, LEMONS, AND RADISH

2 tablespoons olive oil

3 very thin slices lemon, seeds removed, cut into 6 triangles

3 anchovies, chopped

½ clove garlic, finely chopped

3 large radishes, sliced thin (use a Japanese mandolin if you have one) then halved, plus 4 or 5 of the leaves if you have them, sliced

2 tablespoons grated Parmesan cheese, plus more for finishing

Salt and black pepper to taste

A glug of finishing olive oil (optional)

Linguine with Mussels, Chorizo, and Saffron

....

When I went on vacation to Belgium as a child, I ate mussels every day for an entire week. Somehow, I had gotten it in my head that the mussels there were better than anywhere else in the world and so I felt the need to have big, steaming metal pots of them everywhere we went. The dish satisfied a primal fascination with eating with my hands, substituting the cupped shells for a proper spoon. And they came with frites! Thick, golden fries served with mayonnaise totally unlike the jarred kind I knew from home.

I did eventually tire of mussels during that trip, but I still love them, and when cooking them I always pick one out of the pan, spooning up the juices with the shell as I did back then. Here are those steamed mussels of my youth, given an Iberian flair with the addition of chorizo and saffron and served with pasta to make for a heartier meal. Eat with a side of simple vegetables or a salad. I suggest using a fork, but hey, no one's looking …

· Mix the white wine with the saffron in a small cup or bowl and allow to steep. Bring a pot of water to a boil and season amply with salt (it should taste like seawater). When the water is boiling, add the linguine and stir.

· While the pasta is cooking (check the package it came in for timing, and taste it as it gets near—you want it to be very al dente, as it will finish cooking in the mussel juices), heat a 10-inch sauté pan on high and add the olive oil. Add the garlic and stir, then add the saffron-wine mixture plus the tomato and bring to a rolling boil. Add the mussels and shake to distribute in one layer, then cover and cook until they open, about 5 minutes. Remove the mussels to a bowl and cover them to keep warm. If you like, at this point, you can remove the mussels from their shells for easier eating, but it isn't necessary if you've purchased clean, farmed ones. The wild ones will probably need a little rinse inside their cavities to remove any sand.

· Continue to cook the juices to concentrate, another 5 minutes or so. It should look like a chunky sauce, and by this time the linguine should be cooked. Drain and add the pasta to the pan and toss, cooking the pasta into the sauce for another minute. Stir in the chorizo and season to taste with the salt, pepper, and lemon juice. Place in the bowl with the mussels, mix, and top with the parsley.

½ cup white wine

1 pinch saffron

3 ounces linguine

2 tablespoons olive oil

½ small clove garlic, finely chopped

1 small tomato (about 2 inches in diameter, roughly chopped)

1 pound mussels, cleaned (rinsed and, if necessary, debearded)

½ ounce dry Spanish chorizo, sliced thinly into rounds (optional)

Salt and black pepper to taste

Spritz of lemon juice (or to taste)

1 tablespoon roughly chopped flat-leaf parsley

Penne with Broccoli Rabe and Walnuts

Much of what I know about pasta was learned in Paris. Don't discount me just yet—while we made plenty of handmade "pâtes" in my French cooking school, my Italian noodle education came from my friend and fellow culinary student Alex Weinstein, who had previously worked at Union Square Café and a few restaurants in Tuscany and Cortina. This is not to say I'm anywhere near to being a pasta pro (I'm more pasta proficient), but up until that year in France, my experience had been limited to jars of Ragú, and I had never had a meatless pasta that I liked. Alex hosted dinner parties for a group of expat friends at his enormous loft around the corner from my wee apartment in the Marais, and would often serve pasta in a variety of shapes and sauces I never knew existed. This recipe is by no means original. I'm not even sure this is the correct pasta shape for such ingredients. But it is as simple as can be, delicious, and well balanced, and it's perfectly calibrated for a single serving meal.

· Bring a pot of water to a boil and season amply with salt (it should taste like seawater). Add the penne and stir, and boil until al dente (the package it came in should have a time, or taste after 10 minutes or so).

· Heat a 10-inch sauté pan on medium high and add the olive oil. Add the garlic and red pepper flakes and swirl. When just beginning to brown, add the broccoli rabe and 1/3 cup of water, then season with salt and cover. Cook about 2 minutes, then take off the lid, stir in the butter, and remove from the heat. Drain the pasta when it is done, and add to the sauté pan.

· Add the pecorino and lemon zest and toss, then taste and add lemon juice and salt and pepper to taste. Stir in the walnuts and place the pasta in a bowl. Top with more grated pecorino if desired.

3 ounces dried penne

2 tablespoons olive oil

1/2 clove garlic, finely chopped

Pinch red pepper flakes

1/3 bunch broccoli rabe, cleaned and cut into 2-inch pieces

2 tablespoons butter

2 tablespoons grated pecorino cheese, plus more for the top

1/4 of a lemon microplaned for zest

1/2 teaspoon lemon juice, or to taste

Salt and black pepper

1 heaping tablespoon chopped toasted walnuts (roughly 1/4-inch-across pieces)

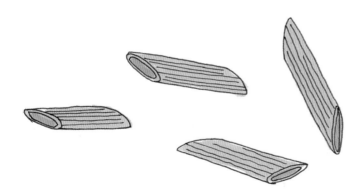

Mac and
Two Cheeses

·······························

The best macaroni and cheese I ever ate was in Paris, when I was interning at the Bistro D'à Côté, Michel Rostang's more casual restaurant. We had it for staff meal one day, and it was perfect: runny, cheesy, and rich, with a crispy, browned top and bits of whole cheese that formed stretchy strings when you removed a spoonful. Before that day, my idea of good mac and cheese was from a box—a processed treat that my mother, when I was growing up in suburban Michigan, would never allow us to have, so when I moved away to school I went a little wild. I still have a little sweet spot for the melted goo that comes in a silver package, but making your own really isn't that much harder, and you can use a nutty, cave-aged Gruyère and a Stravecchio Parmesan to feel more sophisticated and grown up.

· Cook the macaroni per the instructions on the package. Preheat your oven or toaster oven to 400°F (if it has a convection option, use that—it will go faster). In a small saucepan, scald the milk. In another, melt the butter and whisk in the flour and cook on medium-low heat, stirring for 3 minutes. Add the hot milk, a little at a time, whisking constantly, to make a smooth paste. When all the milk is added, bring the mixture to a boil, stirring constantly. Remove from the heat and mix in ⅔ of the Gruyère. When melted, add the cream and season to taste with salt and pepper. Add the cooked macaroni and stir. It should be very saucy.

· I like to just eat it at this point, but if you like a crisp crust, pour the mac and cheese into a small baking dish, then sprinkle the remaining Gruyère on top for that melted stringy effect, followed by the bread crumbs and Parmesan, and bake at 400°F until the top is browned, about 25 minutes.

2½ ounces macaroni

1 cup milk

2 tablespoons butter

1 tablespoon plus 1 teaspoon flour

4 ounces Gruyère cheese, grated

¼ cup cream

Salt and black pepper to taste

3 tablespoons panko bread crumbs (substitute plain bread crumbs) (optional)

1 heaping tablespoon grated Parmigiano Reggiano cheese

"Singapore" Noodles with Shrimp

's ve spent a good amount of time in Singapore. When I traveled around Southeast Asia with my then-partner Jen for just shy of a year, we used Singapore as our hub. It was a place to restock our Western toiletries and refuel in a clean, mosquito- and chewing-gum-free bubble before heading back to rougher, more calamitous locales. In all my visits before and since, not once have I found anything resembling these noodles, which can be ordered from pretty much every Chinese restaurant across America. I haven't been to China as many times, and it's a much larger area to cover, but I'd be willing to wager that these don't exist there either. So are they American? Regardless, with Singapore's rice noodles, fish sauce, and curry powder, these wouldn't be out of place there. Most importantly, they are fast and easy to make, and delicious.

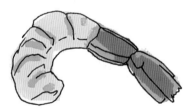

· Heat a 10-inch sauté pan on high. Season the shrimp with salt and pepper on both sides. Add 1½ tablespoons of the oil to the pan and swirl. When just smoking, add the shrimp and turn heat to medium high. When the shrimp is cooked halfway (it will be opaque and reddish on one side), add the snow peas and turn the shrimp. Stir. The snow peas and shrimp should finish cooking at the same time. Ideally, the thickest part at the head end of the shrimp will be a little translucent just at the center, and the snow peas will be a darker green throughout but remain crunchy. Remove to a bowl that you will eat from.

· Add the rest of the oil and the onions to the pan. Turn the heat to medium low. Cook, stirring until translucent, then add the garlic and the curry powder and stir. Add the rice vermicelli (pick it up out of the water with your hands, leaving most of the water behind) and the fish sauce and stir. Cover and cook until noodles are softened, stirring occasionally (this should only take a few minutes). Taste and adjust seasonings, then stir in the shrimp and peas, and replace all in the bowl. Top with the scallions.

4 or 5 medium peeled and deveined shrimp (about 2½ ounces total)

Salt and black pepper to taste

3 tablespoons oil

⅓ cup snow peas or sugarsnap peas (about 8–10 pods)

One ⅓-inch slice medium onion, quartered

½ clove garlic, finely chopped

1 tablespoon curry powder

3 ounces rice vermicelli, soaked in cold water until softened

1 tablespoon fish sauce

1 tablespoon scallion green, sliced

Pork and Squid
Glass Noodles

. . . .

The first time I went to Thailand, I went by myself. I was one year out of college, and Bangkok was the most exotic, compelling place I could think of. Coupled with the allure of white sand beaches, limestone rock formations, food both familiar and new, and its warm, hospitable people, Thailand is an amazing place to be young and alone. This is my version of one of the first meals I had there. *Yum woon sen* is what they call it in Thai—literally, "salad of glass noodles." It's great for warm-weather dining, and its flavor, spicy and exhilarating with lashings of acid from the lime, deeply satisfying from the umami of the pork, squid, and fish sauce, is complex yet comforting—just how I feel about Thailand.

· Bring a pot of water to a boil and season the water amply with salt. In a medium bowl, mix the pork with the light brown sugar, fish sauce, garlic, and a few grinds of black pepper, and set aside. Cook the bean thread noodles in the boiling water, stirring occasionally, until there are no longer any white specks in the noodles and they taste cooked but are not too soft (roughly 3 minutes). Drain and rinse under cold running water, then drain well and place in a mixing bowl (or a larger bowl that you can eat out of).

· Heat a nonstick skillet on high. Add the oil, then the pork mixture and the squid, and stir, breaking up the pork into bits. When cooked through, add to the noodles. Add the remaining ingredients and stir well. Taste and adjust seasonings—you may need a little more salt and pepper to season the vegetables. Enjoy.

¼ pound ground pork

2 teaspoons light brown sugar

1 teaspoon fish sauce

½ clove garlic, pasted

Salt and black pepper

2 small packages bean thread noodles (2½ ounces dry)

2 tablespoons oil

One 5-inch piece squid, cleaned and cut into rings (optional, or substitute 3 pieces shrimp, peeled and deveined, or ½ teaspoon dried shrimp, chopped)

1 tablespoon lime juice

1 teaspoon fish sauce

1 small Thai bird chili, finely chopped (substitute 1 teaspoon Tuong Ot Toi Vietnam chili-garlic sauce), or to taste

1 teaspoon sugar

1 small tomato, chopped, or 4 grape tomatoes, halved

½ Persian cucumber, diced (substitute a 2-inch piece of regular cucumber, or a rib of celery heart)

1 slice red onion, diced

3 mint leaves, torn

3 sprigs cilantro

3 Thai basil leaves, torn

1 heaping tablespoon roughly chopped roasted, salted peanuts

Buckwheat Soba, Salmon, and Salmon Roe Salad

......·.··...........·.··—···....··

'm not a fan of cooking chicken sous vide, as it renders the meat mushy if done too long. But what it does to fish, especially salmon, is nothing short of miraculous! The flesh melts on the tongue, like the Kobe beef of sea creatures. I like to cook my entrée-size salmon filets at 125°F for 8 minutes, but if you don't have sous vide equipment at home, you can approximate the same method by submerging the fish in boiled, salted water (which you have already prepared to cook the soba) and letting it sit at room temperature while you cook the rest of the meal. The water will immediately cool from 212° closer to the 125° range, and while the salmon won't be quite as silky, it will come out perfectly rare inside, and you can just leave it, as the water will cool before the fish gets overcooked. Purists might balk at the water method, as some of the salmon flavor will be lost—but this is home cooking. And they can't see what you're doing, nor do they get to taste the delicious results.

· Bring a small pot of water to a boil and season liberally with salt (it should taste like seawater). Season the salmon with salt and pepper and place in a small bowl. Ladle some of the boiling water over the top until the salmon is fully submerged and allow to sit at room temperature. If the salmon is particularly thick, or if you like it more cooked, you can add another ladle of boiling water after 10 minutes. This should yield salmon that is soft, yet on the rare side.

· Cook the soba per the package instructions, stirring after adding the noodles, then drain and rinse under cold running water. Drain well, and place in a bowl with the remaining ingredients, minus the salmon roe. Taste and adjust seasonings. Remove the salmon from the water and pat dry. Top the noodles with the salmon and the roe. Eat immediately, as soba loses its bite as it sits.

One 3-ounce salmon filet

Salt and black pepper

3 ounces dry soba

1 tablespoon scallion green, thinly sliced on a bias

1 small Persian cucumber, julienned

3 tablespoons dashi

2 tablespoons soy sauce

1½ teaspoons lemon juice

A few gratings of lemon zest on a microplane

2 tablespoons vegetable or other non-flavored oil such as canola

1 shiso leaf (optional)

1 ounce salmon roe

Jap Chae

Before I opened Mirezi, a pan-Asian restaurant on lower Fifth Avenue, the owners sent me to Korean cooking school in Seoul. It was my first overseas work trip, and I was stoked. I was given private lessons by the head teacher at a local culinary academy, a woman in a floral pink apron who might have measured five feet high had she been wearing platform shoes instead of plastic house shoes. All the countertops were proportionately diminutive. Already woozy with jet lag, I had vertigo bending over the worktop—the one time I felt what it must have been like to be Julia Child. One of the recipes we made was *jap chae*, a Korean yam-noodle dish. She showed me how to cut the vegetables exactly the same thickness as the noodles, by shaving sheets off the outer edge of a cylinder of carrot or zucchini with a ten-inch chef's knife, then lining up the sheets and slicing them into thin matchsticks. We painstakingly made the beef strips exactly the same size. Then we assembled the dish. As we were eating, I noticed how easily all the ingredients stayed on the chopsticks; had they been different sizes, they might not have worked as well together—just like this mini chef and her mini counters.

· Mix the sugar and soy sauce together and pour half of the mixture over the strips of beef, add half the garlic, and mix. Season liberally with black pepper. Season the carrots and zucchini separately with salt and allow to sit 5–10 minutes (while you prepare the rest), then squeeze dry. They should exude a good bit of liquid.

· Bring a pot of water to a boil and season amply with salt (it should taste like seawater). Add the noodles and stir. In the meantime, heat a nonstick sauté pan on high and add a tablespoon of the vegetable oil. Add the onions and the carrots and remaining garlic and sauté until wilted. (A little color is okay.) Remove to a bowl. Add the other tablespoon of oil and the beef and stir to separate the strips. Cook through, add the zucchini, stir, and remove to the same bowl.

· Boil the noodles until you no longer see white specks but they are still slippery and toothsome. (I won't tell you to follow the package instructions, as they're usually in Korean—but if they happen to be in English, that's probably a good place to start.) Drain and add to the bowl. Add the remaining soy sauce mixture and sesame oil, mix, then taste and adjust the seasonings with pepper and salt if necessary.

2 tablespoons sugar

2 tablespoons soy sauce

4 ounces beef such as flap, strip steak, or round, cut into thin strips

1 clove garlic, finely chopped

Salt and black pepper

⅓ cup julienned carrots, cut on a Japanese mandolin (medium teeth)

⅓ cup julienned zucchini, cut on a Japanese mandolin (medium teeth)

3 ounces *dang myun* (Korean yam-starch noodles) (substitute bean thread noodles)

2 tablespoons vegetable or other non-flavored oil such as canola

1 slice onion (about ¼ cup)

1 teaspoon sesame oil

Risotto with Summer Squash and Lemon Zest

. . . .

Risotto does require some vigilance, especially when making it for one, but it takes no more than thirty minutes start to finish, including prep time, and it is endlessly versatile. This is a summer recipe, but you can substitute fresh peas in spring, small cubes of butternut squash in the fall, or celery root in the dead of winter. If you are substituting the vegetable and are unsure how long it takes to cook in the rice, cook it separately beforehand, then just stir it in at the end. That, along with the use of a timer, makes this recipe almost foolproof.

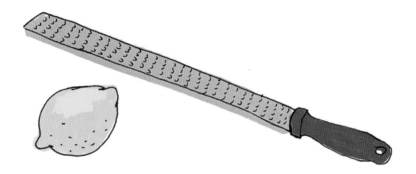

· Heat the stock in a small pot and turn heat to its lowest setting.

· In another pot (you can use a ceramic one you can eat from to save on washing up), melt 2 tablespoons of the butter, then add the shallot on medium heat. Cook, stirring, until shallot is soft and translucent, but not browned. Set a timer for 20 minutes at this point and start it. Add the rice and stir, cooking for about a minute, until the rice is translucent around the edges. Add the wine and reduce, stirring occasionally, until the wine is almost gone. Using a 2-ounce ladle, add the stock, a ladle at a time, stirring constantly and keeping all rice in contact with the stock—don't let errant kernels stick to the side of the pot drying out while the others cook and absorb stock. When the stock is absorbed, add another ladle and repeat the process. Add the squash before the last addition of broth, after 16 minutes (when the timer reads 4 minutes). Taste it at 18 minutes (when the timer reads 2 minutes). In the end, the rice should be al dente—it shouldn't taste raw or stick to your teeth, but each individual grain should have a distinct bite. The risotto should also be creamy and soupy-thick, but not able to hold a shape in the pot. The whole cooking time should not exceed 20 minutes. Stir in the remaining tablespoon butter, lemon zest, herbs, and grated Parmesan, then season to taste with salt and pepper. Top with more Parmesan if desired and serve immediately.

1½–2 cups chicken stock

3 tablespoons butter

1 tablespoon chopped shallot

½ cup arborio, vialone nano, or carnaroli rice

⅓ cup white wine

⅔ cup ½-inch cubes summer squash

A few gratings on a microplane of lemon zest (about ½ teaspoon)

1 teaspoon chopped chives

1 pinch chopped tarragon

2 tablespoons grated Parmesan cheese, plus more for the top

Salt and black pepper to taste

Sticky Rice with Chinese Sausage and an Egg

Pushcart-style dim sum stresses me out. My inner gluttonous child won't let me relax and enjoy the food on my plate while other carts go by and I potentially miss out on something amazing. I get food anxiety. So this recipe is a more substantial version of one of my "can't miss" dim sum favorites, sticky rice in lotus leaves. Mine is made without the lotus leaves and mushrooms, but it is true to the dish's main flavors. It takes a little forethought to make, as it's best if you soak the rice for at least a few hours before cooking, but the prep time is minimal. And when it's done, you can have your sticky rice all to yourself.

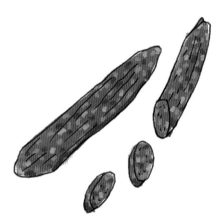

· Place the rice in a heatproof bowl with everything except the edamame, egg, sauce mixture, and scallions. Stir. Allow to sit at room temperature for 1 hour before steaming, or cover and soak overnight, or during your workday.

· Fill a pot big enough to hold the rice bowl with 1½ inches of water and place an elevated rack or ring of tin foil in the center—something to elevate the bowl above the water. Place bowl on top, cover the pot, and bring to a boil, then turn heat to medium low. The water should still simmer. Cook for 25 minutes, then add the edamame and crack the egg over the top, and cook another 7 minutes. Serve with the sauce mixture on the side, topped with the scallions.

½ cup short-grain glutinous rice

1 tablespoon plus 1 teaspoon soy sauce

1 tablespoon Shaoxing cooking wine (the brown-colored one; or substitute dry sherry)

1 tablespoon sugar

2 Chinese sausages, cut into ¼-inch-thick rounds

1 teaspoon chopped small dried shrimp

¼ cup peeled edamame

1 egg

1 tablespoon soy sauce mixed with 1 teaspoon Tuong Ot Toi Vietnam chili-garlic sauce

1 tablespoon scallion greens, sliced on bias

CHAPTER 3

FISH AND SHELLFISH

Alone tonight? Consider the clam. Clams are solitary creatures, living buried in sand, encased in their own shells. The idiom "to clam up" refers to the bivalve's tendency to clap its shell shut when disturbed. But clams are loved across the world as a food source, and in the Northeast, the shells were once used as currency by Native Americans. The Latin name of the hard-shell clam is *Mercenaria mercenaria*, which refers to its use in commerce. And the saying "happy as a clam"? This is shortened from "happy as a clam at high tide"—when clams can't be dug up, and are left alone and content.

As you will be, after preparing this easy, tasty recipe.

. . . . .

· Heat a shallow braiser or pot on medium heat. Add the oil, then the garlic and ginger, and stir until garlic is sizzling but not browned. Add the stock or water, then the clams, and cover. Cook until the clams have just opened. Then, using a slotted spoon, remove them to a warm bowl.

· Add the oyster sauce, sriracha, sugar, pepper, and black beans to the broth in the pot. Bring back to a boil on high heat and whisk in the dissolved cornstarch a little at time until thickened. Spoon sauce back over the cooked clams and garnish with the Thai basil, mint, or scallion greens.

Clams with Chinese Black Beans and Basil

2 tablespoons vegetable or other non-flavored oil such as canola

1 small clove garlic, chopped

1 pinch julienned ginger

½ cup unseasoned chicken stock (or water)

1 dozen littleneck clams or 24 Manila clams, washed

2 tablespoons oyster sauce

1 teaspoon sriracha sauce (optional)

1 teaspoon sugar

Black pepper to taste

½ tablespoon loose Chinese fermented black beans

1 teaspoon cornstarch mixed with 2 tablespoons water

1 tablespoon julienned Thai basil, mint, or scallion greens

New England Clambake

············•··················•··•··•·

When I was little, my family spent summers in Chatham on Cape Cod, and we would often have traditional New England clambakes. It was one of my favorite meals, and I asked for it every birthday back in Michigan, which was somewhat impossible, as steamer clams were hard to come by and my birthday falls in the middle of winter, when corn is at its worst. We stopped going to Cape Cod when I was about eleven, so when I had my first clambake at my Massachusetts boarding school orientation dinner many years later, it felt like I had come home. After I bought my first house on Long Island, I discovered a steamer clam bed on the bay nearby, and I felt the same way. Food evokes a strong sense of place and identity, and this meal—of local ingredients presented in their pure state—is perfect comfort food, embodying the essence of New England.

· Cut any rubber bands off the lobster claws, as this will add a bad flavor to the broth. Add 1 inch of water to a pot just large enough to hold the lobster and other ingredients. Place potatoes in the pot and bring to a boil. Add the lobster, head first. Cook for 3 minutes, then add the littleneck clams and corn and cook another 6 minutes (9 minutes total). If using steamer clams, add during the last 2 minutes of cooking. Season the butter with salt and pepper and melt in a small ramekin placed on top of the lid of the pot while the ingredients are cooking.

· Serve your meal with the bowl of melted butter, a small bowl of the cooking liquid (to rinse your clams in), and the wedge of lemon. You'll need nut or lobster crackers and perhaps a little extra salt.

1 pound live lobster

3 small red-skinned potatoes (1½–2 inches in diameter)

6 littleneck clams (substitute a dozen steamers)

1 ear sweet corn on the cob, shucked

3 tablespoons butter

Salt and black pepper

1 wedge of lemon

Don't Waste It!

Save the remaining liquid and lobster shells to make shellfish broth as you would lobster stock; see page 173.

Barbecued Shrimp, New Orleans Style

·········•·····•···········•··•···•··

Sometimes, nothing short of a lot of butter will do. This is one of those recipes.

You can justify the amount in all sorts of ways: Butter is a key component of Louisiana cuisine. It wouldn't be authentic to have this dish with any less. Butter is a good fat, according to several scientific studies on heart disease. And damn it, it tastes good—the sweetness plays perfectly with any crustacean's oceanic succulence; the fat acts as a direct flavor conduit to the pleasure centers of your soul. In the wise words of Oscar Wilde, "Everything in moderation. Including moderation." Amen.

·   ·   ·   ·   ·

· Devein the shrimp by inserting the tip of a sharp paring knife, blade side up, into the rounded top of the shrimp where the tail meets the head. Cut along the back of the tail, through the top ¼ thickness of the meat, to expose the vein. Remove the vein with your fingers, leaving the shell intact.

- Heat a small sauté pan on high. When hot, add the oil, and when just smoking, add the lemon slices. Brown lemon on both sides, then remove to a bowl. Turn heat to medium high and add the shrimp. Cook on both sides until shrimp is almost but not quite cooked through—the thickest part of the tail near the head end should be just translucent in the very center. Then remove to the bowl with the lemon, leaving 3 of the heads in the pan. The shrimp should be nearly translucent at the center when you take them off the heat.

- Turn heat to medium, add 1 tablespoon butter along with the shallot and garlic and stir. Cook 1 minute, then add the spices and bay leaf and stir again until fragrant. Add the white wine, the Worcestershire Sauce, and the hot sauce and bring to a boil. Press the heads with a fork or spoon to help extract the flavor. Reduce by half, then incorporate the 2 tablespoons of cold butter by adding a little at a time, stirring constantly, until the butter is emulsified into the wine mixture.

- Season to taste with salt, a healthy amount of freshly ground black pepper, and a little lemon juice if necessary, to taste. Add the shrimp back into the sauce and warm through, then remove to the bowl and top with the lemon slices and scallions. Serve with French bread to sop up the sauce.

6 ounces large shrimp (preferably head on), shell on

1 tablespoon oil

2 thin slices lemon, seeds removed

3 tablespoons cold butter, cut into small pieces

1 tablespoon shallot, minced

1 clove garlic, finely chopped

1 teaspoon paprika

1 pinch cayenne pepper

1 pinch dried oregano

1 pinch dried thyme

Pinch Old Bay Seasoning

1 bay leaf

¼ cup white wine

½ teaspoon Worcestershire Sauce (or to taste)

2 teaspoons Crystal Hot Sauce (or to taste, substitute Frank's, or ½ teaspoon Tabasco)

Salt and black pepper to taste

Lemon juice, if necessary, to taste

1 tablespoon scallion greens, chopped

Good French bread, for serving

Shrimp with Cashews and Indian Spices

Something extraordinary happened when I visited the spice market in old Delhi. I was in India with a score of other chefs as well as Divine, a group of three opera singers from Sweden, helping to raise funds for a charity. The market was an assault on the senses. You could hardly move because of the glut of people, rickshaws, cows, and stray dogs. A cacophony of human voices, bells and horns, dogs barking and cows mooing, plus the clang of commerce, threatened to obliterate you. Above, a tangle of electric wires hung like spidery nests, and the scent of a million spices stalked us everywhere we turned. Along with the tropical heat, it was overwhelming, yet thrilling. We were crowded in front of one spice stall—mushed up against it, really—when the three women from Divine started to sing. The palpable power of their voices drowned out all other sounds. Suddenly, the entire market stopped and listened, the music creating order from chaos. I could feel that everyone around me had chills. I believe it actually got colder. Sometimes, the smell of Indian spices brings me back to that remarkable crack in time. Truly Divine.

मसाले

· Heat a small sauté pan on high. Season the shrimp on both sides with salt and pepper. Add 2 tablespoons of the oil to the pan. When smoking, add the shrimp and turn heat to medium high. Cook, turning the shrimp when halfway done (about one to two minutes), then add the tomatoes. When the shrimp is cooked, remove all to a warm serving bowl. The shrimp should be translucent at the center of the head end.

· Add the onions to the pan along with the remaining tablespoon of oil and stir. Cook until soft and translucent, then add the garlic and ginger and stir again. Add the spices and stir. When fragrant, add the stock and scrape the bottom of the pan to release any spices that are stuck, then add the cashews and bring to a boil.

· Put the cashew mixture into a quart container, or the beaker that came with your hand blender, and puree until smooth. Season to taste with salt and pepper and the lemon juice. Pour over the tomatoes and shrimp, top with cilantro, and serve with plain cooked basmati rice.

5 ounces large shrimp, peeled and deveined

Salt and black pepper

3 tablespoons vegetable or other non-flavored oil such as canola

6 grape tomatoes, or one 3-inch-diameter tomato, diced

1 slice onion, chopped (about ¼ cup)

1 small clove garlic, finely chopped

½ teaspoon finely chopped ginger

1 teaspoon *garam masala*

1 teaspoon curry powder

1 pinch cayenne pepper (or to taste)

½ cup lobster or chicken stock, or coconut water

¼ cup roasted cashews

1 teaspoon lemon juice

2 sprigs cilantro (optional)

Cooked basmati rice, for serving (optional)

Fish Stew with Mussels, Fennel, and Chilies

know I'm not alone in wanting to eat sustainably and save our oceans. This recipe is not only healthy for you, it's also healthy for the planet—mussels are one of the fastest-growing proteins available, and they are filter feeders, meaning that they clean the waters around them as they grow. Pairing that with a lesser-known species of fish like porgy or sea robin is heart healthy in more ways than one.

· Heat a small- or medium-size pot on medium heat and add the 2 tablespoons of olive oil. Add the onions and sweat, stirring occasionally, until translucent and soft, about 5 minutes. Add the garlic and red pepper flakes and stir. Add the thyme, fennel, and wine and reduce by ¾. Add the tomato and cook, stirring until the tomato breaks down. Add the clam juice and bring to a boil.

· Season the fish with salt and pepper on both sides. Add the mussels to the pot and bring to a boil again, then add the fish and simmer until almost cooked through (about 1 minute per inch of thickness). Season broth to taste with salt and pepper and lemon juice if necessary. Serve in a large bowl, with the bread on the bottom, garnished with the chopped fennel and another drizzle of olive oil.

2 tablespoons olive oil, plus more to taste

½ small onion, sliced

1 large clove garlic, sliced

½ teaspoon red pepper flakes (or to taste)

1 sprig thyme (or a pinch of dried thyme)

½ fennel bulb, sliced into ½-inch-thick slices, then cut into strips

½ cup white wine

1 approximately 4-inch-diameter ripe tomato, chopped

One 8-ounce bottle clam juice

One 4-ounce firm white fish filet (such as porgy or sea robin)

Salt and black pepper

½ pound mussels, cleaned (rinsed and, if necessary, debearded)

1 teaspoon lemon juice, or to taste

Several slices toasted crusty bread drizzled with extra-virgin olive oil

1 teaspoon chopped fennel fronds

Broiled Bluefish,
Muffaletta Style

Many Long Island fishermen have recounted this bluefish recipe to me: Season a piece of bluefish with salt and pepper and coat it on all sides with jarred mayonnaise. Place on a piece of tin foil and broil, until cooked through, about 8 minutes. Discard the fish and eat the tin foil.

Such is the unfortunate reputation of this plentiful species. But in the right hands, bluefish is one of my favorite local fish. Just caught, quickly bled and iced, its flesh is mild, sweet, and tender, yet rich. My good friend and amazing chef April Bloomfield once served me perhaps the best bluefish dish I have ever had, cut from a thirty-pound monster she had wrestled from the depths of the sea off Montauk. This recipe is based on that memory. The strong flavors of the olive salad play well with the oily fish much better than a jar of mayo.

· Preheat your oven or toaster oven to broil. Rub the bluefish with the teaspoon of olive oil on both sides and season both sides with salt and pepper. Place skin side up on an ovenproof tray, close to the heat source, and cook until skin is lightly browned and crisp and the fish is just cooked through, about 5 minutes, depending on thickness. Use a cake tester or thin knife to test doneness—insert it into the thickest part of the filet, hold there for a solid 3 seconds, then test immediately on your lip. If it is warm to the touch, the fish is done.

· To make the olive salad, mix the ingredients together, taste, and adjust seasonings. To serve, make a bed of the olive salad and place the fish on top.

FOR THE BLUEFISH

One 5½-ounce filet bluefish, skin on

1 teaspoon olive oil

Salt and black pepper

FOR THE OLIVE SALAD

Scant ¼ cup pitted Niçoise or Kalamata olives

Scant ¼ cup pimiento-stuffed queen olives

Scant ¼ cup giardiniera (Italian jarred pickled vegetables), drained and roughly chopped

½ clove garlic, chopped

½ teaspoon anchovy paste

1 tablespoon drained capers

1 teaspoon red wine vinegar

2 tablespoons extra-virgin olive oil

½ teaspoon chopped Calabrian chili condiment (optional)

3 leaves fresh oregano, chopped (substitute a small pinch of dried oregano if you don't have fresh)

6 cubes day-old plain baguette (optional)

Salt and black pepper to taste

· · · · · · ·· ·· ··· ··· ··· · ··· ·· ···· ··

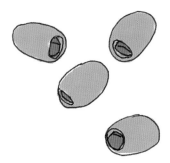

Broiled Bluefish with Avocado, Grapefruit, Pistachios, and Chilies

Bluefish is a prized species in Turkey—so much so that it is overfished and you only see the little "snappers," or six- to eight-inch-long baby fish, that are so plentiful in the Northeast. And it's one of the more expensive fishes there. But many Americans overlook this locally abundant species, or turn up their noses because they find it too "fishy." I can assure you that when it is fresh, there is nothing fishy about it. It's delicious. It is definitely a richer fish, however, and needs the strong acid provided in this dish by the lime and grapefruit. Only buy bluefish from a greenmarket purveyor or fishmonger you trust. I hope this recipe will change your mind about this species.

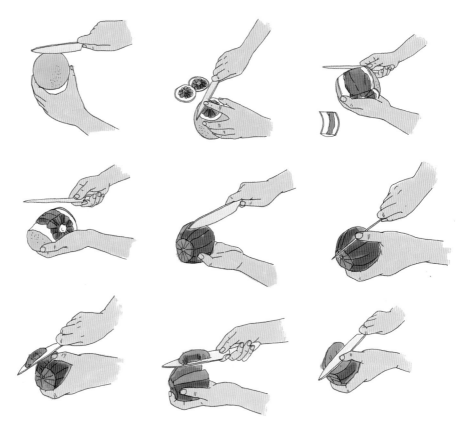

· Preheat the broiler to high. Rub the bluefish with the oil on both sides, then season both sides with salt and pepper. Place skin side up on a small baking sheet close to the flame and cook until skin is browned and crisp, about 4–5 minutes depending on your broiler.

· Remove and allow the heat of the baking dish to finish the cooking. In the meantime, mix the remaining ingredients together, taste, and adjust seasonings. Place on a plate and top with the bluefish. Serve with fresh corn on the cob or corn chips.

Don't Waste It!

Eat the other half of the grapefruit tomorrow for breakfast and use the other half of the avocado for Broccoli Stem Slaw (see page 164).

One 5½-ounce filet bluefish, skin on (substitute other rich fish such as wild salmon)

1 tablespoon olive oil

Salt and black pepper

½ ripe Hass avocado, cubed

½ pink grapefruit, sectioned (see note)

1 heaping tablespoon diced red onion

½ smallish clove garlic, pasted

1 small Thai bird chili, finely chopped, or to taste (substitute ¼ serrano pepper)

Juice of 1 lime

1 tablespoon roasted, shelled pistachios (optional)

Corn on the cob or plain corn chips, for serving

NOTE
To section a grapefruit, cut each end off just enough to expose the flesh, then cut off the rind also just enough to expose the flesh. Run your knife in between the fruit and each membrane to remove each section of grapefruit. Discard any seeds.

NOTE
If using a serrano chili, the remaining pepper can be frozen in a ziplock bag for later use.

Salmon with Mushrooms in Dashi

················•··•···········•··•··•··•···

Recently I went to Alaska to learn about commercial fisheries. We went angling, explored purse seiner and gillnetter ships, visited a cannery, hiked up rivers that were being rebuilt to make them easier for salmon to spawn, kayaked over what seemed to be millions of fish readying themselves for the journey upstream, and visited a local hatchery, where we saw how the eggs were harvested and fertilized (there is a guy whose sole job is to take the male fish by the bellies and squeeze them in order to spew their milt or semen out over buckets of roe) then hatched and cared for into their small fry and fingerling stages. I'm pleased to report that the Alaskan wild salmon population is alive and well, due to the state's careful management practices (and that guy!). The year 2015 marked the state's largest salmon harvest on record. Here's one way to eat them.

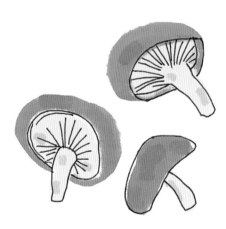

- In a small pot (using a ceramic one you can eat out of will save you a pot to wash), heat the oil over high heat. Add the onions and stir. Cook until lightly browned and caramelized. Add the mushrooms and stir, then add the dashi, soy sauce, and mirin and bring to a boil.

- Season the salmon on both sides with salt and pepper, then add to the pot. Turn the heat to medium and cook until a cake tester or small knife inserted into the thickest part and left there for 3–4 seconds goes in easily and comes out warm. If you want your salmon cooked through, keep going for another 2 minutes or so. Add the bok choy and allow to wilt, then season to taste with the lemon juice and zest and top with the kombu and scallions. Serve with rice.

2 tablespoons oil

Two ⅓-inch slices onion, halved

2 ounces mushrooms such as maitake, cremini, oyster, or shiitake, cut into bite-size pieces

1 cup dashi (see recipe page 172)

2 tablespoons soy sauce

1 tablespoon mirin

One 5½-ounce filet wild salmon (substitute farmed arctic char), skin on or off, depending on how you like it

Salt and black pepper

1 small head Shanghai bok choy, cleaned and separated into leaves

A few drops lemon juice plus a few microplaned grates of zest, to taste

1 square kombu, about 4 x 4 inches, rinsed, left over from dashi recipe, and sliced

1 tablespoon chopped scallion greens

1 cup cooked rice (see recipe, page 150), for serving

Slow-Cooked Halibut with Shishito Peppers and Bread Sauce

· · · · · · · ·•·· ·•··· · · · · · · ·•·•·· ···•·· ·

When I went halibut fishing in Alaska, our guide brought along a handgun. "There's been a few barn doors caught in these waters, and they can kill you," he said, referring to the several-hundred-pound fish, which are about that big. He loaded enormous hooks with a whole small fish, plus a strip of cod and a strip of salmon, about the size of an entrée portion in Texas, added a cannonball weight, and down we sent them, some six hundred feet to the bottom. The bait, hook, and cannonball weight were heavier than any fish I'd ever caught thus far, or so it seemed. We were aiming big.

WHAM!! This was the biggest hit I've ever experienced. Just as soon as it hit, I lost it. Then I lost another, and another. Finally I was able to keep one on, even though my arms were screaming in pain. My whole body was in motion from the fish as it tried to jerk free. It took at least twenty minutes for me to get it to the surface, and I thought I was going to die.

The name halibut comes from the middle English, *hali*, or "holy," and *butte*, or "flatfish," as it was eaten on Catholic holy days. I was certainly expecting a HOLY FLATFISH, something the size of a large cowboy. Luckily we had a pistol. But when it surfaced, it was an innocent-looking fifteen-pound fish— just big enough to be legal to catch. I killed it. No firearms necessary. And it was delicious.

• Use the smallest shallow baking dish or sauté pan that the fish will fit into and add the 3 tablespoons of olive oil, then place in a cold oven or toaster oven and turn to its lowest setting, or 200°F, to preheat. Season the fish with salt and pepper, and when the oven is preheated, place fish in the oil, turning once to coat and leaving the whitest side up. Bake for 5 minutes, then turn off the heat.

• Make the bread sauce: Remove the bread from the water, and drain gently. Place in the container your hand blender came with (or a quart container) along with the garlic, onion, vinegar or lemon, 2 tablespoons of olive oil, paprika, and almonds if using, and blend until smooth. Season to taste with salt and pepper.

• Heat a small sauté pan on high. Add 1 tablespoon of olive oil and, when just smoking, add the shishito peppers. Turn heat to medium high to brown the peppers, then turn and finish cooking on the other side. Season with salt. To serve, place the bread sauce on a plate, then place the shishitos in the center on top, then the fish on top of that. Discard the oil the fish cooked in.

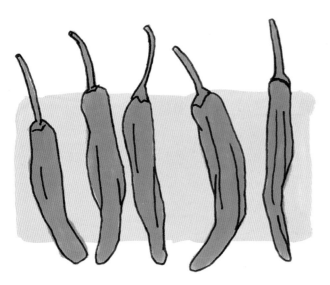

. . . .•.••.•...••..•...••.• ••• •.••.•..• .••

FOR THE HALIBUT

3 tablespoons olive oil

One ⅓-pound halibut filet

Salt and black pepper

FOR THE BREAD SAUCE

1 small slice stale, cubed plain bread such as French baguette, soaked in water (or use 2 tablespoons bread crumbs and 2 tablespoons water)

½ clove garlic

1 thin slice red onion (about a heaping tablespoon)

2 teaspoons red wine vinegar or lemon juice

2 tablespoons extra-virgin olive oil

1 teaspoon paprika

3 salted roasted almonds (optional)

Salt and black pepper

TO SERVE

1 tablespoon extra-virgin olive oil

6 shishito peppers

. . . .•.••.•...••..•...••.• ••• •.••.•..• .••

Whole Roasted Porgy with Grape Leaves, Bulgur, and Lemon

Porgy, aka scup, are a kind of sea bream plentiful off of Long Island, where I have a house. You can often catch several at a time if you set up a rig with a few hooks baited with clams. They eat shellfish and thus are sweet, and are also inexpensive. People say that porgies are bony, but they have the same bone structure as most round fish. Just watch for bones around where the fins attach to the body, and along the top center of the filet. And don't forget the cheek meat. No need to worry about bones there.

Porgy is a lean fish and can get dry if you overcook it, so pay attention. The grape leaves will help keep the moisture in while adding acidity and salinity and should be eaten along with the meat of the fish. If you can't find a porgy, any small, whole, white-fleshed fish will do.

· Preheat a broiler on high. Rinse the fish and pat it dry with a clean paper towel inside and out. Coat with olive oil and season both inside and out with salt and pepper. Place the herb sprigs, garlic, onion slice, and lemon slice in the belly cavity up into the head, then wrap the body with the grape leaves. If you haven't heeded my advice to grow your own herbs and only have one of the herbs I've listed, that's okay—the flavor won't be as complex, but it will still be delicious. Coat with a little more olive oil, then place on a shallow baking dish or sheet tray.

· Bring a small pot of water to a boil. Place the bulgur in a small bowl and season with salt. Pour ⅓ cup boiling water over the bulgur, then cover in plastic wrap and allow to sit at room temperature while you prepare the other ingredients.

· Place the fish under the broiler about 5 inches from the heat source. Allow to cook until browned, about 5 minutes, then flip and finish the cooking on the other side, about another 3 minutes. The grape leaves will be a little charred and a small knife or cake tester should insert easily into the thickest portion of the fish, just behind the head, above the belly cavity.

· Once the bulgur has absorbed the water, fluff with a fork. Mix in the lemon juice, olive oil, tomato, red onion, and parsley. Season with salt and pepper to taste. Serve with the cooked fish, with the wedges of lemon on the side.

FOR THE PORGY

One 1-pound porgy, scaled and gutted, fins removed

Olive oil, to coat

Salt and black pepper

1 sprig thyme

1 sprig tarragon

1 sprig parsley

1 clove garlic, smashed

1 slice onion

1 slice lemon

3–4 grape leaves, large stems removed

FOR THE BULGUR

¼ cup bulgur

Salt and black pepper to taste

1 teaspoon lemon juice

1 tablespoon extra-virgin olive oil

5 grape tomatoes, sliced

1 slice red onion, small dice (about 2 tablespoons)

1 tablespoon flat-leaf parsley, chopped

TO SERVE

2 wedges lemon

Salt-Broiled Spanish Mackerel with Broccoli Rabe and Orange

Spanish mackerel is the mildest tasting of the small mackerels and is meaty and white like swordfish. It is relatively inexpensive and easy to cook—its flesh is forgiving, even when overcooked. It is still a mackerel, however, and thus can stand up to full-flavored ingredients such as bitter broccoli rabe, bracing lemon and orange, and the umami bomb of anchovy. Here these strong ingredients play well together, none overpowering the others.

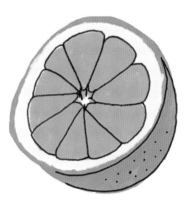

· Preheat a toaster oven or regular oven to broil. Coat the Spanish mackerel with the teaspoon of olive oil and season both sides with salt and pepper. Place on a baking tray or pan.

· Heat a 10-inch sauté pan on high and add the tablespoon of olive oil. Swirl and add the sliced garlic and the red pepper flakes and stir. When sizzling but not browned, add the broccoli rabe and a splash of water (about ¼ cup), then season with salt and cover with a lid.

· Place the fish in the oven as close to the heat source as possible. Remove the lid of the broccoli rabe and stir, and finish cooking while the water evaporates. Remove to a plate and keep warm. Discard any remaining juices and wipe the pan clean with a paper towel.

· Place pan back on the heat and add the 1½ tablespoons of olive oil. Add the red onions and stir until translucent, then add the garlic, anchovies, and red pepper flakes and stir again. Add the orange and lemon zests and juices and reduce until syrupy. Season to taste with salt and pepper, then use the sauce to surround the broccoli rabe (if the broccoli rabe has released some juices, pour this off first), then top with the browned mackerel. Serve with bread or any of the potato recipes in the book.

FOR THE MACKEREL

One 5½-ounce filet Spanish mackerel, skin on

1 teaspoon olive oil

Salt and black pepper

FOR THE BROCCOLI RABE

1 tablespoon olive oil

½ clove garlic, sliced

Pinch red pepper flakes

⅓ bunch broccoli rabe, cleaned (about 3 ounces) and cut into 2-inch pieces

Salt to taste

TO FINISH

1½ tablespoons olive oil

1 slice red onion, finely diced (about 2 tablespoons)

½ clove garlic, finely chopped

1½ anchovies, chopped

Pinch red pepper flakes

Zest of ¼ orange

Zest of ¼ lemon

⅓ cup orange juice

2 teaspoons lemon juice

Salt and black pepper to taste

French bread, for serving

Roasted Arctic Char with Lentils, Hot Dates, and a Cold Shower of Skyr

. . . . ⋅⋅ . ⋅⋅ . . . . ⋅ . ⋅ ⋅⋅ . ⋅ . . . ⋅ . . ⋅⋅ .

I once dated an Icelandic artist for two weeks. I fell hard for her—she was smart, beautiful, and made the most amazing sculptures. On our last date, we took a walk up Riverside Park in Manhattan and found a dead body floating in the river. True story! We followed it for about a half hour as it floated upstream while we waited for the police, the EMT, or the fire department to get there. It turns out that the man had committed suicide by driving his car into the river a few days prior. Afterward, we had dinner in Harlem, and as I was walking her home, she broke up with me. A version of this dish was on my Valentine's Day menu that year. If you're feeling especially bleak, serve this with A Single, Broken Egg on a Bed of Torn, Wilted, Bitter Greens (page 18).

. . . . .

. . . . ⋅⋅ . ⋅⋅ . . . . ⋅ . ⋅ ⋅⋅ . ⋅ . . . ⋅ . . ⋅⋅ .

FOR THE DATES

3 pitted dates

2 slices thick bacon, 1 piece cut into thirds and the other into thin strips about ¼-inch wide

1 small carrot, peeled and sliced into thin rounds

Pinch ground cumin

. . . . ⋅⋅ . ⋅⋅ . . . . ⋅ . ⋅ ⋅⋅ . ⋅ . . . ⋅ . . ⋅⋅ .

· Wrap each date in a piece of the bacon and secure with a toothpick. Bake on a tray in a 375°F oven or toaster oven along with the strips of bacon and the carrots in a single layer under the dates until hot and bacon is crispy in parts, about 6–8 minutes. Move dates to the side, add the pinch of cumin to the carrots and bacon, and stir.

· To make the lentil salad, mix the cooked sliced bacon and rendered fat with the cooked carrots, lentils, herbs, onions, garlic, vinaigrette, and salt and pepper. Mix. Taste and adjust seasoning as desired.

· Mix the skyr with the garlic, lemon juice, and salt and pepper. Taste and adjust.

· Heat a sauté pan on high. Season the fish on both sides with salt and pepper. Add the oil to the pan and when just smoking, add the fish, skin side down. Turn the heat to medium high and cook until skin is browned and crisp, about 4 minutes. Turn and finish cooking to desired temperature. Serve on a bed of the lentils, with the skyr drizzled on top, and garnish with the dates.

FOR THE LENTILS

1 slice bacon from above

½ cup French green lentils, boiled and drained

1 pinch chopped thyme leaves

1 pinch chopped tarragon leaves

1 pinch chopped chives

1 tablespoon finely diced red onion

½ small clove garlic, pasted

2–3 tablespoons mustard vinaigrette (recipe page 157)

Salt and black pepper to taste

FOR THE SKYR

3 tablespoons plain skyr (Icelandic yogurt) (or substitute any plain yogurt)

½ small clove garlic, pasted

1 teaspoon lemon juice

Salt and black pepper to taste

FOR THE ARCTIC CHAR

One 5½-ounce filet arctic char

Salt and black pepper

2 tablespoons vegetable or other non-flavored oil such as canola

Sautéed Filet of Fluke with Corn, Basil, and Clams

·······.··..············.··™·····...··

This is a simple summertime dish that's easy enough for a weeknight dinner for one, but nice enough to serve if you feel like having guests. You can dress it up by making a garlic-basil puree instead of using sliced basil. Remove the corn with a slotted spoon once the butter is added and stir the puree into the remaining juices to make a bright green sauce.

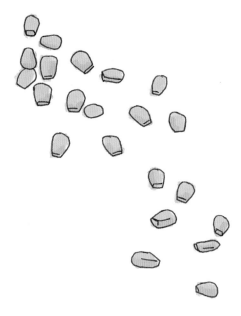

· In a small sauté pan, bring the stock or water to a boil and add the clams. Cover and cook until the clams open. Discard any clams that do not open and remove the rest to a warm bowl. Take out of the shell if desired. Place the corn in the remaining stock and bring to a boil. Add the butter and stir until the butter is emulsified into the stock. Season to taste with salt and pepper. Stir in the basil. Surround with the clams and keep warm while you sauté the fish.

· Heat a sauté pan on high for 2 minutes or until hot. Season the fish with salt and pepper on both sides (it is usually a thin filet, so go light), then dust lightly with the flour. Add the oil, and when smoking, add the fish, whitest side down. Immediately turn heat down to medium high. Cook until lightly browned, then turn over the fish, count to 12, and place on top of the corn. Spritz well with lemon juice and enjoy.

2/3 cup lobster stock, chicken stock, clam juice, or water

5 Manila or small littleneck clams, washed

1 ear sweet corn, kernels removed from cob (cut into a large bowl to save the mess)

2 tablespoons butter

Salt and black pepper

2 large leaves basil, thinly sliced (about a tablespoon)

One 5-ounce filet fluke, skin off

Wondra flour for dusting (substitute regular flour)

2 tablespoons vegetable or other non-flavored oil such as canola

Spritz of lemon juice

Boston Mackerel, Cucumber, and Avocado Hand Rolls

....·......··...........··.·.·...··

f your heart needs healing, feed it some omega-3 fatty acids. Boston mackerel (also known as Atlantic mackerel) has about two times the omega-3s of wild king salmon at a tenth of the cost. In the spring and fall, the fish are fat and delicious, as long as you have a reliable fishmonger or sushi counter that can sell you fresh product. In this recipe, the fish's fat is balanced by the vinegar and the powerful flavors of the ginger, onion, and garlic. Wrapped in shiny nori paper, these hand rolls are like little gifts for your health.

· Place the rice wine vinegar, garlic, and onion in a small shallow tray, then nestle the fish, skin side down, in the mixture. Allow to sit in the refrigerator while you julienne the cucumber, chop the scallion, and slice the avocado. Set them aside.

· Season the fish on both sides with black pepper. Use either a blow torch to lightly char the skin, or place the fish skin side down on an oiled rack and place the skin directly into the fire of your gas burner on high (try not to cook the flesh, just the skin). If you have neither of these, just peel off the top layer of skin and discard—it should come off easily after sitting in the vinegar. Slice the fish.

· Make hand rolls with a few slices of fish, a bit of rice, a slice of avocado, a few pieces of cucumber, a pinch of scallion, and a piece of ginger wrapped in half sheets of nori. Dip in the soy sauce, eat, and repeat.

2 tablespoons rice wine vinegar

1 clove garlic, sliced

1 slice onion

One 5½-ounce filet Boston mackerel, skin on, sushi quality

1 small Persian cucumber, julienned on a Japanese mandolin

1 scallion, thinly sliced

½ ripe Hass avocado, sliced

Black pepper

1 cup cooked sushi rice

A few slices Japanese pickled ginger (jarred)

3–4 sheets nori, toasted

2 tablespoons soy sauce, for dipping

Roasted Filet of Hake with Spinach-Potato Gratin

Hake is a sweet, cod-like fish perfect for baking. The flavors of this dish are the same as those of *brandade*, a salt cod–potato puree, and one of my favorite dishes that I learned in cooking school in France. Spinach makes this a balanced meal, and the bread crumbs add texture, as well as being an economic, ecological way to use up old bread.

· Preheat the oven to 400°F. Position two racks so one is in the center of the oven and the other is around 5–6 inches from the broiler. Season potato slices with salt and pepper and toss with the onions and most of the garlic (save just a pinch), and place in a small, shallow baking dish (a 3 x 5-inch one would be ideal—you're looking for something where the potatoes will come up maybe 2/3 of the way to the top—this could also be a very small ovenproof sauté pan). Cover with the cream and bake on the middle rack for 25 minutes.

· In the meantime, prepare the spinach and the fish. Bring a pot of water to a boil, add some salt, and then add the spinach. When the spinach is wilted, drain and refresh under running cold water. Squeeze dry to form a ball. Roughly chop and reserve.

· Mix the bread crumbs with the remaining garlic, the thyme, and the olive oil and season to taste with salt and pepper. Season the fish with salt and pepper on both sides, then top the whitest side with the bread crumb mixture.

· Remove the gratin and turn the oven on broil. Add the spinach to the gratin, pushing to submerge it in different parts to distribute evenly, lifting a layer of potato if necessary. Top the gratin with the fish and replace in the oven on the upper rack. Bake until the bread crumbs are browned and the fish is just cooked through, about another 8 minutes for a 1-inch-thick filet. Spritz with a little lemon before eating.

1 Idaho potato, about 8 ounces, peeled and sliced on a Japanese mandolin into 1/8-inch-thick rounds

Salt and black pepper

1 slice onion, halved

1 small clove garlic, finely chopped

1/2–2/3 cup cream

1 handful spinach (2 ounces), washed, any large stems removed

2 tablespoons plain bread crumbs

Pinch fresh thyme leaves

1 tablespoon olive oil

One 1/3-pound hake filet, skin off (substitute pollock or Alaskan cod or haddock)

Lemon wedges, for spritzing

Steamed Sea Bass with Shiitake

This is a version of my go-to dish for dining alone. It's a sized-down adaptation of one of my mother's recipes from childhood (okay! I miss my mommy when I'm alone) with the addition of shiitakes for some extra umami (pun intended) to fill the void.

· · · · ·

One 5½-ounce filet sea bass, skin on, skin lightly scored with a knife to prevent curling

Salt and black pepper

1 dried shiitake mushroom, soaked in warm water, stem removed, cap sliced

2 tablespoons vegetable or other non-flavored oil such as canola

3 tablespoons soy sauce

1 whole scallion, chopped

1 teaspoon julienned ginger

Plain steamed rice, for serving

· Season the sea bass lightly on both sides with salt and pepper. Place in a small, shallow baking dish and add remaining ingredients.

· Redistribute solid ingredients so they evenly cover the top and bottom of the fish. Add 1 inch of water to a pot large enough to fit the baking dish inside. Add an elevated grate or a ring of tin foil to raise the baking dish above the water. Bring the water to a boil, then add the baking dish, and cover. Steam for 5 minutes or until a paring knife is easily inserted into the thickest part of the filet. Serve with plain steamed rice.

CHAPTER 4

POULTRY

Grilled Breast of Chicken with Banana Pepper Dip and "Fattoush"

Disclaimer: I am not single. (Believe it or not!) But it's hard to meet someone when you're a chef. Dating can only happen on irregularly scheduled days off, or in the wee hours of the morning after work. Then there's the fact that most of us are neurotic perfectionists, not to mention that many of us use the professional kitchen to hide the fact that we're socially inept. So the good news is that I am presently with another chef, and feel lucky to have a partner. I feel even luckier that her father is Lebanese and her mother makes this banana pepper dip every time we visit. Make extra and eat it for a snack on pita bread—or, better yet, if you can find it, the Lebanese flatbread, *markouk*.

FOR THE CHICKEN

Olive oil

1 boneless chicken breast
(around 5½ ounces), skin off
and reserved

Salt and black pepper

FOR THE DIP

1 large banana pepper, seeded
and sliced (substitute Anaheim
chili, or ½ yellow bell pepper
with some habanero for heat),
about 2 ounces

1 tablespoon olive oil

2 heaping tablespoons feta,
plus 2 tablespoons brine

Salt and black pepper to taste

. . . .··. .. . . · ·. . . . . ·. .

· Grease a small plate with a little olive oil. Season the
chicken skin with salt and pepper and lay it flat, flesh side
down, on the plate. Cover loosely with a paper towel and
microwave on high for approximately 2½–3 minutes, until
the skin is browned and crisp. Alternately, heat a small
sauté pan on high and add a tablespoon of oil. When hot,
add the skin and turn the heat to medium. Cook until
browned and crisped through, turning once during the
cooking and using a spatula to keep it flat. Remove to a
clean paper towel. Cut into triangles and reserve.

· Heat a clean grill or grill pan on high. Coat the chicken
breast on both sides with a little olive oil, then season
both sides with salt and pepper. I like to season the thicker
side a little more heavily and the thinner a little less so
all is perfectly seasoned. Place on the grill and allow to
cook for approximately 2 minutes, or until grill marks are
clearly visible but the flesh isn't burning. Turn the breast
45 degrees and cook for another 2 minutes, then flip and
finish cooking on the other side, about 3 minutes. Check the
thickest part of the breast for doneness. The meat should no
longer appear translucent at the center, but should also still
be juicy.

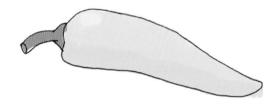

· In the meantime, make the banana pepper dip (this can also be done up to 3 days in advance if you like): Sauté the sliced peppers with a little olive oil until soft and lightly browned. Puree with the feta and its brine, ideally with an immersion blender fitted with the little chopper attachment. It should be like hummus in texture. Add salt and pepper to taste.

· Finally, make the fattoush. It's easy—just mix all of the remaining ingredients except the pita together in a bowl, and toss. Taste and adjust seasonings.

· To serve, place a swipe of the feta mixture on the side of a plate and top with the chicken breast. Place the fattoush salad on the other side and use the chicken skin as if it were pita to scoop it up. (If you're not into crispy chicken skin and want some carbs, toast some pita triangles and use that instead.)

FOR THE "FATTOUSH"

1 small tomato, diced, or 4 grape tomatoes, halved

1 small Persian cucumber halved and sliced, or ¼ cup seeded and cubed regular cucumber

1 slice red onion, diced

5 pitted Kalamata olives

3 large leaves mint or flat-leaf parsley, torn

½ small clove garlic, pasted

1 teaspoon lemon juice

1 tablespoon extra-virgin olive oil

1 pinch sumac powder (optional)

Salt and black pepper to taste

½ piece pita bread, cut into bite-sized triangles and toasted crisp, optional

Grilled Breast of Chicken with Cumin, Lime, and Chilaquiles

. . . .·· . . . . ·.·· · . . . . ··

Chilaquiles is a Mexican breakfast dish made with leftover tortillas and is thus perfect for cooking for one. (Even though it is also traditionally served at the end of a Mexican wedding party, we'll focus on its efficiency and economy.) You can use other types of salsas from what I suggest—tomatillo or mole are also traditional. And you can add other toppings, such as ripe avocado slices or Mexican pickles (see recipe page 000). If you're feeling more Cal-Mex, add a few small pieces of fresh mozzarella when you add the crisp tortillas for a little oozy cheese action.

. . . . .

. . . .·· . . . . ·.·· · . . . . ··

FOR THE CHICKEN

1 boneless, skinless chicken breast, pounded to even thickness

2 tablespoons lime juice

½ large clove garlic, finely chopped

1 large pinch ground cumin

1 large pinch red pepper flakes

1 tablespoon olive oil

Salt and black pepper

. . . .·· . . . . ·.·· · . . . . ··

· Marinate the chicken breast by mixing it with the lime juice, garlic, cumin, and red pepper flakes in a small bowl or dish.

· Preheat the oven or toaster oven to 350°F. Cut the tomato in half and coat with the teaspoon of olive oil, then season with salt and pepper. Bake in the oven on a small tray, cut side down, until softened (about 10 minutes), then remove the skin (they should just slip off). In the meantime, remove the stem and seeds from the guajillo chili and cover with warm water to soften.

· Brush the tortillas with the olive oil lightly on both sides and season with salt. In the oven, toast the tortillas directly on the rack, until lightly browned and crunchy, about 7 minutes.

· Puree the softened guajillo and baked tomato together with the garlic and pinch of oregano, using your hand blender and some of the guajillo soaking water. In a small sauté pan, heat the tablespoon of olive oil and sauté the onions on medium heat until translucent. Add the tomato mixture and cook until a little thickened, then season with salt and pepper to taste.

· Heat a grill or grill pan on high. Remove the chicken from the marinade and coat with a little olive oil, then season with salt and pepper. Place on the grill and cook for 2 minutes or until nice brown grill marks are formed, then turn 45 degrees and cook another 2 minutes. Flip and finish cooking on the other side, about another 3 minutes.

· Break the tortillas into triangles, add to the tomato sauce, and toss while simmering until some of the sauce is absorbed. Place on a plate next to the finished chicken and top with the queso, crema, and cilantro.

FOR THE SALSA

1 small tomato (about 2 inches in diameter), hard stem part removed

1 teaspoon olive oil plus 1 tablespoon

Salt and black pepper to taste

1 dried guajillo or New Mexico chili (substitute canned chipotle and skip the rehydrating step)

½ large clove garlic

1 small pinch oregano

1 slice onion, diced

Salt and black pepper

FOR THE TORTILLAS

3 corn tortillas

Olive oil

Salt

TO SERVE

2 tablespoons crumbled queso fresco or grated queso anejo

1 tablespoon crema or sour cream (optional)

2 sprigs cilantro (optional)

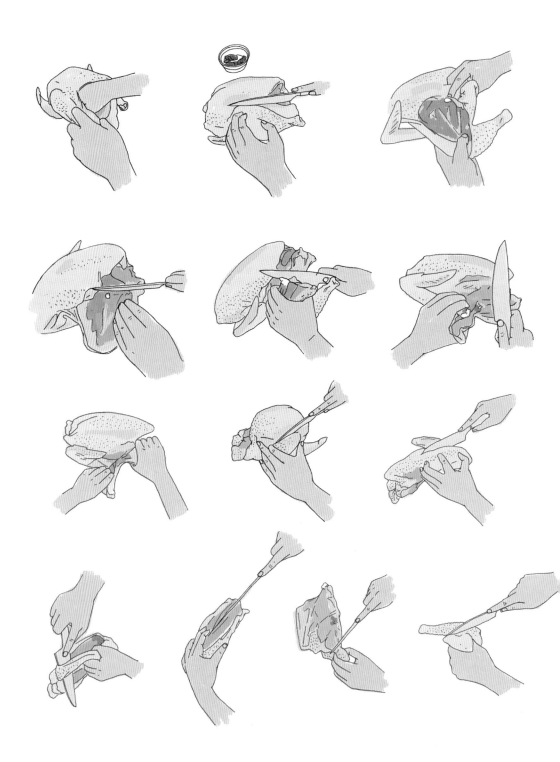

· See recipes (pages 87–104). Place one 3½- to 4-pound chicken on a cutting board breast side up. Remove bag and place neck and gizzards in a pot.

· Remove wing forearms by cutting through the elbow joint. Or remove the entire wing starting at the armpit and slicing up through the joint that holds it to the ribcage. Be careful to leave the breast meat intact.

· Remove legs by first slicing through the skin that connects them to the breast, closer to the leg so as to leave skin covering the whole breast. Using your hands, push the leg away from the breast, out and down toward the cutting board to dislodge the thigh bone from the hip. Then separate the thigh from the backbone by running a knife from the tail portion just next to the back until you cut through the hip joint.

· Do not attempt to remove the oyster (the small round muscle in the back, at the top of the thigh) with your knife. Using your hands, rip the leg free. The oyster should come free from the back cleanly. Repeat with the other leg. Place 1 leg and 1 wing each in quart ziplock freezer bags or seal with your FoodSaver and freeze for later use.

· Remove the breasts. Locate the breastbone with your fingers and cut just to the side straight down toward the cutting board. When you reach bone, angle the knife 45 degrees away from the breast bone and continue until the bottom part is free. Follow the bone up toward the wing, then remove the entire breast by slicing through the joint that attaches the upper wing to the body cage. Repeat on the other side. Place the carcass in the pot with the neck bone and gizzards and follow the recipe on page 170 for chicken stock.

Pan-Roasted Chicken Breast with Roasted Broccoli Panzanella

······.··········.··**··.....

This recipe is a great way to use up old bread. Day old, week old, two weeks old—as long as it isn't moldy, it will work. The lemon and olive oil soaks into the dry bread to make it soft and delicious again. And paired with the chicken breast, you have a balanced meal that covers all four food groups.

· · · · ·

Don't Waste It!

·······································

Get a basil plant. You'll have something to take care of! Or make pesto with the rest and freeze it.

· Preheat oven to 425°F. Mix broccoli with 2 tablespoons of the olive oil, then season with salt and pepper. Place on a baking sheet and put in the oven. In the meantime, heat a sauté pan (preferably ovenproof) on high. Pat the chicken dry using a clean paper towel, then season with salt and pepper on both sides. Add 2 tablespoons of olive oil to the pan and, when smoking, add the chicken, skin side down. Leave on the heat for 30 seconds, then place the sauté pan with the chicken in the oven with the broccoli. (If you don't have an ovenproof pan, just place the chicken in a separate roasting dish.) Bake 5–6 minutes or until skin is browned, bubbly, and crisp, then turn. Turn the broccoli at this point as well. Bake another 6 minutes, until just cooked through. Remove both the broccoli and the chicken and set aside on a warm plate. The broccoli should be browned in places. Cut into bite-size pieces.

· In a large bowl, mix the lemon juice and anchovy paste with the garlic and whisk in the remaining 3 tablespoons of olive oil. Add the red pepper flakes, basil, and red onions, then the bread cubes and broccoli, and toss. Taste and adjust seasoning as needed. Serve with grated Parmesan over the top alongside the chicken.

1 small head broccoli, florets cut off, stems saved for another use

7 tablespoons olive oil

Salt and black pepper

1 chicken breast, skin on

Juice and zest of ½ lemon

½ teaspoon anchovy paste

1 small clove garlic, pasted

Pinch red pepper flakes

3 large leaves basil

2 tablespoons diced red onion

1½ cups loose cubed stale French bread

Freshly grated Parmesan cheese

Pan-Roasted Breast of Chicken with Caramelized Onions, Bacon, Liver, and Frisée

There was a café down the street from my cooking school in Paris that had the most delicious chicken liver salad. It really was just a few pieces of sautéed liver with a classic green salad that you probably could get at any café in Paris, as they all had similar menus. But for me, this particular one is steeped in nostalgia. My fellow students and I would sit in the window box after school, drinking *"demi pressions"*— small beers on tap—and eating lightly (as we had already had what we had made that day in class), laughing and feeling more cosmopolitan than we actually were. Here are those flavors, dressed up for a full meal.

· Heat a sauté pan on high. Pat the chicken breast dry with a clean paper towel. Season it along with the liver with salt and pepper on both sides. Add the oil to the pan and when just smoking, add the chicken breast, skin side down, and the liver. Turn heat down to medium high, and cook until skin is browned, crisp, and bubbly. The liver should be done first—turn when it is browned and finish cooking on the other side, then remove to a small bowl. Turn the chicken breast, turn heat down to medium, and cook until the meat is opaque throughout at its thickest part, about 12 minutes start to finish. Remove to a plate and place on top of the bread, cut side up to catch the juices.

· Place the frisée in a mixing bowl along with the thyme leaves, olive oil, and mustard. Pour out any excess oil from the pan and wipe out any blackened bits with a clean paper towel. Add the bacon to the sauté pan and render, then remove with a slotted spoon to the bowl with the frisée, leaving the rendered fat in the pan. Add the onions to the pan and cook until all is browned and soft. Remove to the bowl with the liver and mash with a fork to form a thick paste. If you prefer a smoother texture, you can chop it finely on your cutting board or buzz it with your hand blender. Use this liver puree to top the bread that the chicken has been sitting on, then dot with the chopped prune. Add the red wine vinegar and the thyme branch to the sauté pan and turn off heat, scraping to remove any bits that have stuck to the bottom. Remove the branch and discard, then pour the vinegar over the frisée. Season with salt and pepper and mix, then serve with the liver toast and cooked chicken breast.

FOR THE CHICKEN

1 chicken breast, bone in and skin on, wing tip attached

1 chicken liver

Salt and black pepper

2 tablespoons vegetable or other non-flavored oil such as canola

One 3-inch portion baguette, halved and lightly toasted if not fresh

FOR THE FRISÉE

2 ounces frisée lettuce, washed (you can substitute mesclun)

1 sprig thyme, leaves and branch separated

1 tablespoon extra-virgin olive oil

1 teaspoon Dijon mustard

1 slice bacon, cut into ¼-inch-thick strips

2 slices onion, halved (about ½ cup)

1 prune, roughly chopped

1 tablespoon red wine vinegar

Smothered
Chicken Leg and
a Biscuit

....

To smother is to mother with an "s." It doesn't work so well in relationships, but it does wonders when you're cooking, resulting in a comforting stew that mothers the soul. This dish is smothering in its most basic form, using ingredients I generally have on hand, but some mushrooms wouldn't be out of place, nor would some fresh fava beans or ramps if they are in season.

· · · · ·

· Preheat an oven or toaster oven to 350°F. If it has a convection option, use it.

· **FOR THE CHICKEN:** Heat a small, heavy-bottomed pot on high. Season the chicken pieces with salt and pepper on both sides. Add the oil to the pot and when just smoking, add the chicken pieces, skin side down. Turn heat to medium high, and cook until nicely browned, then turn and brown the other side. Remove to a plate and turn heat to medium low.

· Pour off the excess oil. Add the butter and melt, then add the onions and carrots and stir, scraping the bottom of the pot to remove any browned bits. Cook for 2 minutes, then sprinkle in the flour and stir. Cook for 2 more minutes, then slowly stir in the stock. Add the chicken back to the pot along with any accumulated juices, cover, and turn heat to low. It should simmer with the lid on. Check occasionally and stir so the sauce doesn't burn.

· **FOR THE BISCUIT:** In a small bowl, mix the flour, sugar, baking powder, and salt together, and cut in the butter. Rub the mixture between your hands until it has a sandy texture and to incorporate the butter. Add the cream and form into a dough, but don't overmix. Place on the toaster baking sheet in a round, flattened mound, about 1 inch high, and bake until risen and golden browned all over, about 15–20 minutes (but in a convection oven it will cook faster).

· Remove the lid on the chicken pot when your biscuit is about halfway done and turn up the heat if necessary so it simmers. Allow to reduce until nicely thickened. Once the biscuit is done, remove from the oven and allow to cool. Add the peas, lemon zest, and tarragon to the chicken pot, and season to taste with salt and pepper. Serve with the biscuit.

FOR THE CHICKEN

1 chicken leg (drumstick and thigh separated)

1 chicken wing

Salt and black pepper

2 tablespoons oil

1½ tablespoons butter

1 slice onion, chopped (around ¼ cup)

3 cups carrot, cubed

1 tablespoon flour

1 cup chicken stock

¼ cup peas

Pinch lemon zest (grated on a microplane if you have it)

5 leaves tarragon, chopped

FOR THE BISCUIT

½ cup flour

½ tablespoon sugar

1 teaspoon baking powder

Pinch salt

.8 ounces butter (or, if you must, a generous 1½ tablespoons)

¼ cup cream

Chicken Tagine with Couscous

A tagine is a North African clay cooking vessel with a conical lid that catches the steam and funnels its condensation back into the stew. The traditional dish that is cooked in a tagine has come to be called the same thing—no matter what kind of pot you use. Here I give my version of this braise. I've modeled it after my memory of several couscous dishes I had at Chez Omar, a Moroccan restaurant I frequented when I lived in the 4th arrondissement in Paris. I've included easy-to-find vegetables, but pumpkin, sweet potato, and chickpeas are classic additions. Serve it with harissa to make it spicy (get it in a jar or a tube—canned is harder to keep—and refrigerate after opening).

· Heat a small pot or Dutch oven (or traditional tagine, if you have one!) on high. Season the chicken pieces with salt and pepper on both sides. Add the olive oil to the pot and when just smoking, add the chicken, skin side down. Turn heat to medium high and lightly brown chicken on both sides. Remove to a bowl and turn down heat to medium.

· Mix the wine and the saffron together and allow to steep while you start the stew. Add the onions to the pot and stir. Cook, stirring occasionally, until soft and translucent, but not browned. Add the garlic and stir. Add the saffron wine and tomato and reduce by ¾, about 5 minutes, depending on the size and shape of your pot. Return the chicken back into the pot along with any juices and cover with chicken stock, then add the cinnamon and bring to a boil. Skim and turn to a simmer. Add the carrots. Cook for 25 minutes.

· In the meantime, make the couscous: Place in a small bowl with a pinch of salt. Bring a small pot of water to a boil and pour ⅓ cup over the top of the couscous. Cover with plastic wrap and allow to sit at room temperature. Add the zucchini and raisins, if using, to the pot and bring back to a boil. Season to taste with salt and pepper. Fluff the couscous with a fork before serving and eat with the stew with a dollop of harissa mixed in, if desired.

FOR THE CHICKEN

1 chicken leg, thigh and drumstick separated

1 chicken wing

Salt and black pepper

2 tablespoons olive oil

½ cup white wine

Pinch saffron

1 slice onion, quartered (about ¼ cup)

½ clove garlic, chopped

One small tomato, chopped

Chicken stock to cover (about 1½ cups, substitute water)

½ small stick cinnamon

¼ cup cubed carrot (substitute turnip)

FOR THE COUSCOUS

¼ cup couscous

Pinch of salt, plus more to taste

½ cup cubed zucchini

1 teaspoon raisins (optional)

Black pepper

Harissa (optional)

Thai
White Curry
with Chicken

Spice up your life! Make it fiery, sweet, and rich with a balanced complexity ... at least for dinner. This weekday stew is endlessly adaptable as well as being quick and easy. Substitute any protein for the chicken and vary the vegetables with the season. Variety is healthy for the body as well as the soul.

. . . . .

Don't Waste It!

See recipe on page 190 for what to do with leftover coconut milk.

· Heat a saucepot on medium. Season the chicken with salt and pepper. Add the oil to the pot and when hot, add the onions and stir. Cook until translucent, then add the garlic and the Thai bird chili and stir again.

· Add the seasoned chicken and the root or longer-cooking vegetables such as bell peppers, if you are using them (green vegetables will be added later). Stir. Add the coconut milk, the lemongrass, and the lime leaf and turn heat to medium high. Cook until the vegetables and chicken are cooked through and the coconut milk has thickened. Add green vegetables at this point, plus the fish sauce and sugar, and bring back to the boil. Season to taste with salt and pepper, stir in the basil, and serve over rice.

1 boneless, skinless chicken thigh (or breast), cut into thin 2-inch strips

Salt and black pepper

2 tablespoons vegetable or other non-flavored oil such as canola

1 slice onion, cubed (around ¼ cup)

½ clove garlic, finely chopped

1 Thai bird chili, finely chopped (or to taste)

1 cup mixed vegetables such as eggplant, carrots, peas, red bell peppers, broccoli stem matchsticks, etc.

½ can coconut milk (use an unsweetened pure brand such as Chaokoh, and freeze the rest for another use)

One 2-inch piece lemongrass, pounded (crushed)

1 kaffir lime leaf

1 tablespoon fish sauce

1 tablespoon plus 1 teaspoon sugar

3 large leaves Thai basil, torn (optional)

Cooked rice, for serving

Oyako Don

You might be wary of a dish called "parent and child over rice," as this classic chicken and egg dish is called in Japanese, but you shouldn't overlook it, because it is easy to make and delicious. It will be even more savory if you buy a chicken that's lived a good life and eggs from one as well. Besides, you should know where your food comes from—a fact that this dish's name drives home—literally!

· Heat a small pot on high. Add the oil, and when smoking, add the onion slices and stir, then turn heat to medium high. Cook until caramelized and wilted.

· Season the chicken leg meat with salt and pepper and add to the pot. Stir. Add the dashi, soy sauce, mirin, and bok choy and bring to a boil. Turn to a simmer, then pour in the beaten egg, cook 1 minute longer, and turn off the heat. The egg should just set from the remaining heat. Serve over rice topped with the scallions.

2 tablespoons vegetable or other non-flavored oil such as canola

2 slices onion, quartered (around ½ cup)

1 chicken leg, meat cut from the bones and cut into cubes around 1 inch square

Salt and black pepper

¾ cup dashi (recipe, page 172)

2 tablespoons plus 1 teaspoon soy sauce

1 tablespoon plus 1 teaspoon mirin

1 small head bok choy, cleaned, bottom cut off

1 egg, beaten, seasoned with salt and pepper

Cooked short-grain rice, for serving

1 tablespoon scallion greens, thinly sliced

Japanese Ground Turkey Curry with Apples and Spinach

················•···•.....···•··•··•·•··•··•··•·•··

This recipe has accrued a lot of frequent flyer miles. It originated in India, came to Britain during colonial rule, and then returned to Asia—specifically, Japan—during the Meiji period by way the Anglo-Japanese Alliance. Oddly, the Japanese thought of curry as "Western," and indeed in this recipe the Western influence can be seen in the form of a butter and flour roux. I've added spinach to make it a more balanced meal. You can certainly make it with processed Japanese curry cubes, but those come with all sorts of preservatives and MSG, and this is only slightly more work and very much worth the effort

· Heat a small pot on high. Add the oil, and when just smoking, add the ground turkey in one layer. Season with salt and pepper. Cook until browned, then stir.

· When cooked through, remove to a bowl with a slotted spoon. Pour off any remaining oil and wipe the pot with a paper towel. Turn heat to medium and add the butter. Melt and add the onions and carrots. Cook, stirring, until the onions are lightly browned. Add the garlic, ginger, bay leaf, and apple and stir. Whisk in the flour and cook for 2 minutes or until the raw flavor is cooked out. Add the curry powder and stir until fragrant. Slowly whisk in the chicken stock to form a thickened, smooth sauce. Add the soy sauce and the cooked turkey and bring to a boil. Add the spinach and wilt, then season to taste with salt and pepper. Serve over cooked rice with the red pickled ginger on the side.

2 tablespoons vegetable or other non-flavored oil such as canola

5 ounces ground turkey

Salt and black pepper

2 tablespoons butter

2 slices onion, chopped (about ½ cup)

⅓ cup carrot pieces, about ½ inch thick

½ clove garlic, finely chopped

½ teaspoon grated ginger

1 bay leaf

3 tablespoons peeled, finely diced apple

1 tablespoon flour

1 tablespoon curry powder (use S&B brand if you want it to be really Japanese)

1 cup chicken stock

½ tablespoon soy sauce

1 handful washed spinach leaves

Cooked rice, for serving

Red pickled ginger (optional)

Breast of Long Island Duck with Hoisin and Grapes

. . . .

This is a Westernized version of Peking duck that doesn't involve inflating a whole bird, dousing it with boiling water and a maltose mixture, and drying overnight. In twenty minutes—as long as you begin with a boneless duck breast— you can have crispy skin with sweet hoisin sauce. If you'd like to simplify even further, buy some Chinese steamed buns, omit the grapes and water, and sandwich slices of the breast into the reheated bread slathered with hoisin sauce and garnished with cucumber slices and scallion.

· Score the skin of the duck breast by sliding a knife along it in equidistant lines, and cutting through about ⅔ of the way to the flesh so the skin stays in one piece. Turn and make cross-hatching lines using the same technique. Heat a sauté pan on high for a good minute. Season the duck with salt and pepper on both sides. When the pan is hot, add the duck, skin side down, and immediately turn the heat to low. As fat accumulates, pour excess from the pan. You will need to degrease the pan several times before the duck is fully rendered. When the skin is browned, crisp, and shrinking back from the meat, turn the heat to medium high. Turn the duck over, add the butter and five-spice powder, if using, and baste the breast with the melted fat using a spoon. Finish cooking to desired doneness (1 minute after turning for my preferred medium rare depending on the size of the bird) and remove to a warm pan. Pour off excess fat from the pan and add the grapes. Cook until warmed through and turn off heat.

· Mix the hoisin sauce with the water and sesame oil. Spread on a plate, top with the duck, and garnish with the grapes.

1 boneless duck breast, skin on

Salt and black pepper

1 tablespoon butter

Pinch Chinese five-spice powder (optional)

6–8 seedless grapes (any kind will do)

2 tablespoons hoisin sauce

1 tablespoon water

A few drops sesame oil

Breast of Long Island Duck with Duck Fat Potatoes and Figs

One thing the French and the Chinese have in common is their frugality. Nothing goes to waste in either cuisine. Both practices were born from poverty, which is perhaps why they are so great—food needed to be manipulated to taste good. Historically, good ingredients were scarce in both countries, so all parts of a prized ingredient such as an animal were put to good use. Here is a French-inspired dish that makes use of the rendered fat. Even my grandmother would approve.

· Preheat an oven or toaster oven to 400°F. Season the potatoes with salt and pepper and mix with the garlic and thyme in a small heatproof baking dish that will fit in your oven. Score the skin of the duck breast by sliding a knife along it in equidistant lines, cutting through about ⅔ of the way to the flesh so the skin stays in one piece. Turn and make cross-hatching lines using the same technique. Heat a sauté pan on high for a good minute. Season the duck with salt and pepper on both sides. When the pan is hot, add the duck, skin side down, and immediately turn the heat to low.

· As the fat accumulates, pour excess from the pan into the potato dish, mix, and place in the oven. You will need to degrease the pan several times before the duck is fully rendered, so continue to add it to the potatoes. When the skin is browned, crisp, and shrinking back from the meat, turn the heat to medium high. Allow to crisp a bit, then turn and finish the cooking on the other side to desired temperature (about another minute for my preferred medium rare). Remove to a plate and keep warm. Pour excess fat from the pan, add the port and vinegar, reduce until syrupy, then whisk in the butter. (If you are using dried figs, add them with the port and vinegar so that they soften.)

· Add any accumulated juices from the duck plate and bring to a boil. Use to sauce the plate. By now, the potatoes should be soft and cooked through. Remove to your plate, leaving most of the fat behind. Garnish with the fresh fig halves, if using.

FOR THE POTATOES

3–5 fingerling potatoes, sliced ½ inch thick if large (about 5 ounces)

Salt and black pepper

½ clove garlic, finely chopped

1 sprig thyme

FOR THE DUCK

1 boneless breast of duck, skin on

Salt and black pepper

½ cup port wine

1 tablespoon red wine vinegar

1 teaspoon butter

2 small fresh figs or 1 large, halved (you can substitute dried figs, but add them earlier, as mentioned below)

Duck with
White Beans
and Kale

On a cold day you can cuddle up with this warm, hearty stew, which takes its cues from the southwest of France. It has a generous, robust personality, and it is easy and forgiving. Give it some space. If you take your time with it—letting it heat gently, checking in every once in a while—it will become tender, and will make you feel whole again.

· Heat a medium pot on high. Season the duck pieces with salt and pepper on both sides. Add the olive oil to the pot and swirl, then add the duck, thick-skin side down. Turn heat to medium high and brown, then turn and brown the other side. Turn heat to medium and add the onions. Stir and cook until the onions are translucent, then add the garlic and stir.

· Add the wine, bay leaf, and thyme and cook until the wine is reduced by 2/3, then add the chicken stock and cover. Bring to a boil, cover, and leave to simmer over medium-low heat. Check to make sure there is still liquid in the pot (if it has dried up, add a bit more) at occasional intervals for about 40–45 minutes, or until the duck meat is soft. Add the beans and the kale and cook another 5 minutes. Season to taste with salt and pepper, and enjoy.

1 duck leg, skin on, trimmed of excess fat and skin

1 duck wing

Salt and black pepper

1 tablespoon olive oil

About 1/3 cup chopped onion

1 clove garlic, thinly sliced

1/2 cup white wine

1 bay leaf

1 sprig thyme

1 cup chicken stock (or duck stock)

One 15-ounce can white beans, drained and rinsed well

1 handful kale, washed and sliced (about 1 ounce)

Duck Ragù

T his recipe is quite a project. It is not difficult, but it will take an evening to cook. At the end, though, you'll have several meals at the ready, just from what many people would discard.

Four-legged animals such as beef and pork would be more classic for a ragù, but the dark meat from duck makes a perfect substitute. This is *cucina povera*, or frugal cuisine, at its essence.

This recipe makes 4–5 entrée portions of sauce

· · · · ·

· Place a large pot over very low heat. Cut up the duck fat into small dice and add to the pot in one layer. Allow to render slowly, until the bits are just starting to crisp. This can take up to an hour, but check on it from time to time while you chop your vegetables. There should be crispy little bits of fat at the end, plus around 3 tablespoons of rendered oil.

· Add the butter to the pot, along with the onions, carrots, and celery, and turn heat up to medium low. Cook, stirring occasionally, until the vegetables are browned, very soft, and reduced in size. Add the garlic and tomato paste, and cook another minute. Add the nutmeg, bay leaf, and milk and reduce until dry. Add the red wine and reduce again until almost dry.

· Add the duck carcass, neck, wing tips, heart, and giblet (but *not* the liver), plus the tomatoes, then add chicken stock (or water) to cover. Simmer for 1 hour, keeping the bones submerged by adding more water if necessary, then remove bones, neck, wings, and heart and allow to cool slightly. Remove meat from the bones—there should be quite a bit from the neck, plus some on the carcass. Chop the heart into a fine dice and add all back into the mixture. Simmer, stirring occasionally, for 3–4 hours (or more if you have time—you can even cook it the next day too, by cooling and refrigerating overnight, then reheating to a simmer the next day), or until the sauce is thickened and the fats are pulling away from the tomatoes.

· Puree the liver with a little more stock with a hand blender and stir it back into the still-simmering sauce. Remove the giblet (it should be soft at this point) and chop into bits, then return to the sauce. Season to taste with salt and pepper. Divide into cup containers and allow to cool, then cover and freeze if not using immediately. Reheat in the microwave and serve over tagliatelle or pappardelle, tossed with a little butter and showered with grated cheese.

Duck fat from the inside of the cavity

1 tablespoon butter

1 cup onion, finely diced

2/3 cup carrot, finely diced

2/3 cup celery, finely diced

3 cloves garlic, finely chopped

1 heaping tablespoon tomato paste

A few gratings of nutmeg

1 bay leaf

1 cup milk

1 cup red wine

1 duck carcass, cut up, with the neck, wing tips, heart, giblet, and liver removed

One 28-ounce can peeled tomatoes

Chicken stock (or water), about 2 quarts

Salt and black pepper

TO SERVE

Tagliatelle (see recipe page 32) or pappardelle, cooked and tossed with a little butter, allow 4 ounces per serving

Grated Parmigiano Reggiano cheese

Broiled Squab with Roasted Carrots and Carrot Top Zhoug

Y ou people eat too much chicken. I know this because every cookbook editor I've ever met asks for more chicken recipes. This one did! Overcrowded chicken factories? Hormone-pumped superbirds? Your fault! Okay, maybe it is our collective responsibility as a culture. And I know, guilting people into trying a new food rarely works—but squab is rich and delicious and has been eaten since ancient times in places all over the planet. That many people can't be wrong. While it's a little expensive and harder to find, making it at home costs a fraction of what you'll be charged at any fine-dining establishment, and it's available at the click of a button online if you can't find it at a local specialty grocery store. This recipe celebrates where this bird perhaps was first eaten—in the Middle East. And it makes use of carrots and their tops in the spicy Middle Eastern condiment, *zhoug* or *zhug*, depending on where in the Middle East you might find yourself. Of course, if you must, you can substitute a Cornish hen, which is really just a little chicken, and cook it for a bit longer, about 10–12 minutes, depending on the size.

· Preheat your oven or toaster oven to 350°F. Using scissors, cut through the back of the squab between the legs and wings and lay flat on a plate. Pat the bird dry with a paper towel and rub in the ½ clove garlic, cumin, lemon juice, and olive oil. Allow to marinate at room temperature while you prepare the other ingredients.

· Toss the carrots with ample olive oil, then season with salt and pepper and bake on a small tray until browned and soft, about 20 minutes. Sprinkle the caraway seeds over the top for the last 5 minutes of cooking.

· Meanwhile, make the *zhoug*: Place ⅓ cup of the washed carrot tops, roughly chopped, into the container that your hand blender came with, along with the cilantro, jalapeño, garlic, cumin, coriander, and olive oil and puree with the hand blender until smooth. Add a tablespoon of water to the mix if needed to get the blades going. Season to taste with salt and pepper.

· When carrots are done, keep warm in tin foil, or on top of the toaster or oven while you broil the squab. Turn the oven to broil and season the squab on both sides with salt and pepper, leaving any excess marinade on the plate. Place squab on a tray, skin side up, and broil, 4 inches from the heat source, until skin is browned and crisp and meat is medium rare, about 6 minutes. (Squab, unlike mass-produced chicken, is safe and better served medium rare.) Serve with the carrot top *zhoug*, carrots, and some warm pita, or Chickpeas in Tomato (page 160).

FOR THE SQUAB

1 squab, semi-boneless, about 8 ounces

½ clove garlic, chopped

½ teaspoon cumin

1 tablespoon lemon juice

1 tablespoon olive oil

Salt and black pepper

FOR THE CARROTS

1 bunch baby carrots (or ½ bunch adolescent ones), tops removed but leaving ¼ of green attached to the carrots

2–3 tablespoons olive oil

Salt and black pepper

1 large pinch caraway seeds

FOR THE *ZHOUG*

1 bunch baby carrot tops, washed (substitute parsley for the tops if your carrots didn't come with them)

2 tablespoons chopped cilantro

1 tablespoon chopped jalapeño (or to taste: if your jalapeño has no heat, you can try a serrano, or add a little cayenne)

½ clove garlic

1 large pinch ground cumin

1 large pinch ground coriander

2 tablespoons olive oil

Salt and black pepper

Pita bread, for serving

Red-Cooked
Duck Leg
Over Rice

. . . .••. .•. . . . .••. .••. ..•. . ..

My mother used to make this when I was growing up. She'd use other meats too: chicken or cuts of pork used for braising, the meat falling off the bone and the fat rich and yielding. Sometimes she'd add hard-boiled eggs, which would become brown on the outside as the dish cooked, with a deep, umami-laced flavor. Or she'd add pieces of fried tofu, which would suck up the juices and take on the flavors of the meat. Sometimes there were bamboo shoots for crunch. The leftover liquid could be used for the next red-cooked meat, making a deeper flavor still. But all of it, any way she made it, was delicious over rice.

. . . . .

. . . . . .••. ...•. . . . .•••. . .•. ..•. . ..

1 duck leg, skin on, trimmed of excess fat and skin

1 duck wing

½ cup soy sauce

1 cinnamon stick

1 piece star anise

2 pieces dried shiitake mushroom

One ¼-inch slice ginger

1 scallion white, trimmed

2 teaspoons sugar

Cooked white rice, for serving

1 tablespoon scallion green, sliced

. . . .••. .....•. . . . . .•••. . .•. ..•. . ..

· Place the duck pieces, soy sauce, spices, shiitake, ginger, scallion whites, sugar, and 3 cups of water in a pot and bring to a boil.

· Skim, turn to a simmer, and cook 45–55 minutes, or until soft. When it's finished, the braising liquid should be reduced by about half. Serve over the rice garnished with the scallion.

CHAPTER 5

MEAT

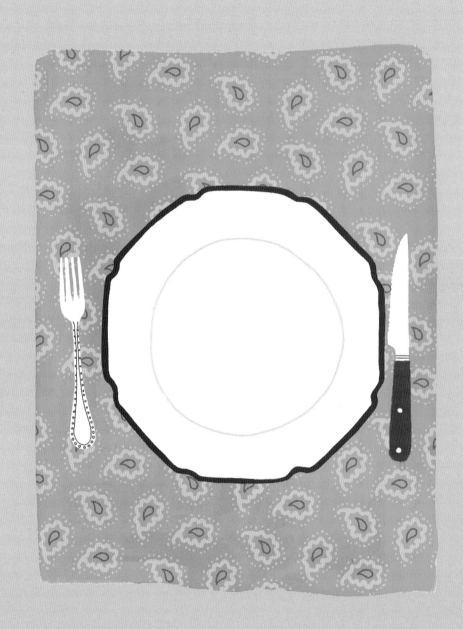

Stir-Fried Pork Belly and Kimchee with Egg

've had this numerous times in Japanese late-night *izakayas*, but even though kimchee is a key ingredient in this dish I've never seen it in a Korean restaurant. I wonder why? Regardless, it is one of the easiest dishes to make, and if you have a Korean or Japanese supermarket around, they usually sell pork belly pre-sliced. The rice will take the longest to prepare, unless you've already made a big pot and can reheat some.

· · · · ·

· Heat a sauté pan on medium high and add the oils. Add the pork belly and season with salt and pepper. Cook until reduced in size and no longer pink, then add the kimchee and soy sauce, and sauté.

· Make a well in the center of your pork mixture and crack an egg into it. Cook until the white is opaque and the yolk is still runny. Season the egg with salt and pepper. Serve the whole thing over cooked short-grain rice garnished with the scallion greens.

1 tablespoon vegetable or other non-flavored oil such as canola

1 teaspoon sesame oil

5 ounces pork belly, rind off, thinly sliced (substitute other fatty pork)

Salt and black pepper

2/3 cup kimchee

1 teaspoon soy sauce

1 egg

Cooked rice, for serving

1 tablespoon scallion greens, thinly sliced

Eggplant
Ma Po Doufu
Style

When I went off to college, my mother sent me a package of index cards with some of her easiest recipes handwritten on them. Ma Po Doufu was one of them. Perfect for a college student, the dish could be made for about a dollar a portion. It quickly became a standard and a favorite of my then-girlfriend Deirdre. Here is an eggplant version, made with one of my favorite condiments, Lao Gan Ma (see page 208). Stir-fry some green vegetables, make a pot of rice, and call it dinner.

Eggplant Ma Po Doufu Style

1 Japanese eggplant —
halved lengthwise, then cut
into 2/3" thick half moons

Salt
3 tablespoons oil
2 ounces ground pork
1/2 clove garlic, fine
1/2 tablespoon ginger
1 tablespoon Lao Gan Ma chili sauce

· In a small bowl, mix the cornstarch with the chicken stock or water and set aside.

· Sprinkle the cut eggplant with the salt and allow to sit while you prepare the other ingredients, then blot dry with a clean paper towel. Heat a 10-inch sauté pan on high (a nonstick one would be good for this, but is not essential), and add the oil. When just smoking, add the eggplant and shake to make one layer. Turn heat to medium high and cook until lightly browned, then stir. Add the ground pork, crumbling it as you go, then add the garlic and ginger and stir. Add the Lao Gan Ma and the soy sauce and stir again. Then add the cornstarch slurry and cook for 2 minutes, stirring, until it is translucent and thick. Garnish with the scallions and serve over plain cooked rice.

1 tablespoon cornstarch

1/3 cup sodium-free chicken stock or water

1 Japanese eggplant, halved lengthwise, then cut into 2/3-inch-thick half moons (approx. 6 ounces)

Salt

3 tablespoons oil

2 ounces ground pork

1/2 clove garlic, finely chopped

1/2 teaspoon ginger, grated

1 tablespoon Lao Gan Ma chili sauce

2 tablespoons soy sauce

1 tablespoon scallion greens, sliced

Plain cooked rice, for serving

Pork and Garlic Chive Dumplings

So, you have nothing to do on a Friday or Saturday night? Why not make an investment in your future? Sure, making your own dumplings is time consuming, but you have plenty of that, and you'll be rewarded with a well-balanced, home-cooked meal in a plump little package that can be ready in minutes for upcoming nights when you don't feel like cooking—this recipe makes enough for excellent leftovers for your freezer. The folding is a meditative exercise. For each dumpling, think of all the good things you want for yourself in the future. If you're not too bitter, think of all the qualities of a perfect mate. When you run out of ideas, think of all your best aspects—you really don't need a partner to complete you. They say positive thinking can ameliorate your future. Shape dumplings and your life—both can be delicious.

Chop the cabbage

Pulse until finely chopped

Peel ginger using the back of the knife

Mix it with your hands

¾ pound green cabbage

½ pound ground pork

¼ pound peeled, deveined shrimp, chopped

½ bunch scallions, finely chopped

½ cup chopped garlic chives (optional)

1 large clove garlic, finely chopped

½ teaspoon grated ginger

3 tablespoons soy sauce

½ teaspoon sesame oil

1 tablespoon sugar

Salt and black pepper to taste

1 package dumpling wrappers

· · · · · ··•·•·· ··· ···· · ·•••· ··•··· ·••·

· Roughly chop the cabbage and place in a food processor. Pulse until finely chopped but not pureed. Remove and squeeze in a clean kitchen towel to remove juices and place dried cabbage in a large bowl for mixing. Add the pork, shrimp, scallions, chives, garlic, ginger, soy sauce, sesame oil, sugar, and salt and pepper and mix. Test for flavor by poaching or frying a small amount, and adjust seasonings.

· To wrap the dumplings, place a tablespoon of filling into the center of each wrapper. Wet the edges, and fold in half, to form a taco-like shape. Make a pleat on the side facing you, about 20 degrees from the apex of the half circle formed by the dumpling skin, toward the top, and seal with your fingers to the back side of the skin. Repeat on the other quarter, in mirror fashion, and seal the dumpling completely, trying to eliminate any air pockets. Place on a sheet tray lined with parchment paper, pleated side up, with dumplings spaced so as not to touch one another. Cover both the wrappers and the folded dumplings with a clean damp cloth to prevent drying while wrapping.

· Repeat until you've used up all the filling, Freeze unused dumplings by placing the entire sheet pan uncovered in the freezer. When frozen, transfer dumplings to a ziplock freezer bag.

· To make the dipping sauce, mix together the rice vinegar with the soy sauce, scallion, sesame seeds, and black pepper.

· Steam the dumplings for about 5 minutes or until cooked through if just made, and 6 minutes if frozen, and serve with the dipping sauce. To pan-fry, heat a nonstick sauté pan over high heat. Add oil to pan and swirl, then add the dumplings in one layer so they don't touch. Add enough water to cover the dumplings halfway, then cover the pan. Cook over medium-high heat until all water is evaporated and the bottoms are browned and crispy.

FOR THE DIPPING SAUCE

3 tablespoons rice wine vinegar

4 tablespoons soy sauce

1 teaspoon thinly sliced scallion white

1 pinch toasted sesame seeds

Ground black pepper to taste

2 tablespoons soybean oil or other non-flavored oil such as canola, for pan-frying

Stir-Fried Greens with Garlic (see page 152), for serving

Slow-Cooker Pork Stew with Tomatillo and Chilies

My dishwasher at annisa, Dion Flores, was from Puebla, Mexico, and made this chile verde one day for staff meal. It was one of my favorites of the year, but unfortunately he never made it again. It was the one-night stand of dinners. But I've re-created it here so you can revisit it, like an old friend.

· Season the pork with salt and pepper. Heat a slow cooker (a small one is better, if you have it, for small portions) on high and add 2 tablespoons of the olive oil. Add the onions and cook, stirring occasionally, until soft and translucent. Add the garlic and cumin and stir. Add the pork and the chicken stock (it should cover the meat), cover, and cook on low for 8 hours, while you sleep or go to work.

· When the meat has finished cooking and you are ready to prepare the dish, puree the tomatillos with the jalapeño (capsaicin levels, or what makes jalapeños spicy, vary greatly from pepper to pepper, so add it a bit at a time and taste as you go—the end result should be a little spicier than you want the resulting stew to be, as it will be diluted a bit from the meat and cooking juices), garlic, and cilantro until smooth using the chopper attachment to your hand blender. Season to taste with salt and pepper.

· Bring ¾ cup water to a boil, then slowly whisk in the masa harina. Cook until thickened and smooth, whisking occasionally, for about 8 minutes. Stir in the remaining 1 tablespoon of olive oil and season to taste with salt and pepper. Keep warm.

· Remove the lid from the slow cooker. The stew should have reduced so that there is about ½ cup of braising liquid left. Stir in the tomatillo mixture and bring back to a simmer. Season to taste with salt, pepper, and the lime juice. Serve the stew over the masa harina.

6 ounces pork stew meat, cubed (pork shoulder works well here)

Salt and black pepper

3 tablespoons olive oil

2 thick slices onion, chopped (about ⅔ cup)

½ large clove garlic, chopped

1 large pinch ground cumin

3 cups chicken stock or water

Two 2-inch-diameter tomatillos, hulled and roughly chopped

½ small jalapeño, or to taste

½ clove garlic

1 heaping tablespoon chopped cilantro

¼ cup masa harina

1 teaspoon lime juice

Grilled Pork Chop with Rosemary, Garlic, and Fennel

The first time I had porchetta, the roasted pork dish from central Italy, I thought it was the best pork I'd ever eaten—and it had been sandwiched between two pieces of focaccia, wrapped in a cocktail napkin, and stored in my then-partner Jen's pocket for the better part of a night before I tasted it. It had been made by an old Italian chef from Rome who came in just for Jen's friend's fiftieth birthday. Made from a whole pig, it was moist from self-basting with bits of crackly skin from which burst tiny jets of fat flavored with garlic, rosemary, and fennel pollen. You would never make porchetta for one—it needs a night to sit with its seasonings, then hours on a spit over a wood fire. But you can have the flavor approximated here in this recipe. Buy the best pork chop you can get—one with good marbling will help mimic the richness of the original dish.

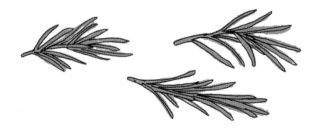

· Rub the pork chop with the rosemary, garlic, fennel pollen, and olive oil evenly on both sides. Heat a grill or grill pan on high (make sure it is clean and well oiled). Season the pork chop with salt and pepper on both sides. Grill for about 1½ minutes, then turn 45 degrees and grill another 1½ minutes. Flip and finish the cooking on the other side, another 2 minutes for medium. Remove and let rest in a warm spot.

· In the meantime, place the fennel in a single layer in a sauté pan along with the lemon and orange juices, butter, and sugar and sprinkle with salt. Pour water over the top to come up halfway and bring to a boil on high. Cook for approximately 5–7 minutes total, turning the fennel when the liquid has evaporated by half, and continue to cook until water is fully evaporated and the fennel is caramelized. Serve with the pork chop.

1 bone-in pork chop, 1 inch thick, about 8 ounces

½ teaspoon chopped rosemary

1 small clove garlic, finely chopped

1 teaspoon fennel pollen (substitute fennel seed, roughly chopped)

1 tablespoon olive oil

Salt and black pepper

½ small bulb fennel, sliced ½ inch thick

1 teaspoon lemon juice

1 tablespoon orange juice

1 tablespoon butter

Pinch sugar

Grilled Vietnamese-Style Pork Cutlet

·······•·····•·····•··•···•··•·•··

All over Vietnam, wafts of wood smoke imbued with the scent of caramel and the deep funk of fish sauce abound. Small portable tabletop grills sit on outdoor tables of many of the restaurants. Whether made with squid or cuttlefish, chicken, beef, or pork such as in this popular dish, Vietnamese barbecue is easy to love.

· Place the pork cutlet on a small tray and mix with the fish sauce, sugar, lemongrass, garlic, and black pepper, turning to coat all sides evenly. Allow to marinate at room temperature while you prepare the other items.

· Bring a pot of water to a boil and season amply with salt. Boil the rice vermicelli per the package instructions (usually about 3 minutes) and drain. Refresh under cold running water and drain well. Place in a shallow bowl that you will eat from. Top with the cucumber, tomato, and herbs.

· Meanwhile, make the dressing: Mix the lime juice, fish sauce, sugar, garlic, Thai bird chili, and water together and keep on the side.

· Heat a clean grill or grill pan on medium high and rub it with an oiled paper towel. Scrape any excess marinade from the pork, then rub with a little oil on both sides and very lightly season with salt. Grill about 1½–2 minutes per side, then slice and place on top of the rice noodles. Pour the lime dressing over the top and eat.

5 ounces pork shoulder or pork chop, thinly sliced (or pounded), about ¼–⅓ inch thick

1 tablespoon fish sauce

1 tablespoon sugar

One 2-inch piece lemongrass, thinly sliced

⅔ clove garlic, finely chopped

8 grinds of black pepper

Salt

2½ ounces rice vermicelli

½ Persian cucumber, sliced

One small tomato cut into wedges, or 6 grape tomatoes, halved

5 leaves of mint or 6 leaves cilantro

Oil for coating

FOR THE DRESSING

1 tablespoon lime juice

2 teaspoons fish sauce

2 teaspoons sugar

⅓ clove garlic, finely chopped

A few thin rounds Thai bird chili

3 tablespoons water

Pan-Roasted Veal Chop with Mushrooms and Oysters

This is a much simplified version of a dish I had on the menu at annisa. It takes its cue from an ancient recipe that paired veal and oysters. I found it online while perusing old English menus hoping to find inspiration, and there it was: *Œyſtreſ æŋđ Veel*—or something like that. It is good for a cold fall or winter night when you want to treat yourself.

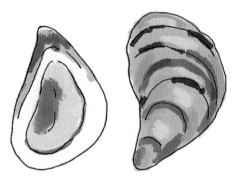

· Heat a sauté pan on high. Season the veal chop on both sides with salt and pepper. Add the oil to the pan and swirl. When the oil is just smoking, add the veal chop. Turn heat to medium high and brown for about 2½ minutes (for a 1-inch-thick chop), then turn and brown the other side for approximately another 2½ minutes for medium rare. Remove to a plate and keep warm.

· Pour the excess oil from the pan and add the mushrooms in one layer along with the butter and season with salt and pepper. Cook until browned on one side, then add the shallot and stir. Add the chicken stock and stir, scraping up any of the browned bits stuck to the bottom of the pan. Add the cream and reduce until thickened. Add the thyme and any juices that have accumulated around the veal and bring to a boil. Turn off the heat and add the oysters (if using) and stir. Allow to just heat through, then taste and adjust the seasoning of the sauce, adding a little lemon juice if the sauce seems too rich. Pour the sauce over the veal chop and eat, ideally with a steamed artichoke.

One 8-ounce bone-in veal chop

Salt and black pepper

2 tablespoons vegetable or other non-flavored oil such as canola

2 ounces mushrooms, cleaned (such as oyster, maitake, or cremini)

1 tablespoon butter

1 teaspoon shallot, finely diced

3 tablespoons chicken stock (substitute white wine)

3 tablespoons heavy cream

Pinch thyme leaves

2 oysters, shucked (optional)

A few drops lemon juice (less if using wine instead of chicken stock)

Steamed artichoke, for serving (page 154, optional but delicious)

Kibbe with
Tahini Sauce

My girlfriend's father taught me how to make *kibbe naye*, which is a traditional Lebanese dish of raw beef or lamb. He makes it for special occasions in a big loaf and serves it with sweet onion slices for scooping it up. The next day, he uses the remaining meat to make a cooked version much like the following.

· Preheat an oven or toaster oven to 375°F. Place the bulgur in a small bowl and add 2 tablespoons and 1 teaspoon boiling water (any more water and it gets too wet; any less and it gets too crunchy). Cover with plastic wrap and allow to steep for approximately 5 minutes.

· In the meantime, make the tahini sauce: Mix together the tahini, lemon juice, garlic, and salt and pepper with 1 tablespoon of water and set aside.

· Place the ground beef in a bowl along with the onions, cinnamon, allspice, lemon juice, olive oil, and bulgur. Season to taste with salt and pepper and mix together, then press into a small baking dish to form a patty around ½ inch thick. Place in the preheated oven and bake until cooked through, about 12 minutes.

· To eat, stuff portions of the kibbe into lettuce wraps and drizzle with the tahini sauce..

FOR THE KIBBE

2 tablespoons medium bulgur

5 ounces ground beef or lamb

1 slice red onion, finely diced (about 3 tablespoons)

1 large pinch cinnamon

1 large pinch allspice

1 teaspoon lemon juice

1 tablespoon extra-virgin olive oil

Salt and black pepper to taste

FOR THE TAHINI SAUCE

2 tablespoons tahini

1 tablespoon lemon juice

½ small clove garlic, pasted

Salt and black pepper to taste

TO SERVE

1 small head bibb lettuce, washed

Korean-Style Flanken Lettuce Cups

..........··....··........····...··....··

The best thing about eating alone is you can hog everything. Korean restaurants are wonderful—they're communal and interactive, and you get to taste a million different things. But you have to share. Here's a recipe for when you want to eat more than your portion of *kalbi*: rich, tender beef ribs, sliced thin, with a caramelized depth from sugar and soy and a hint of char from the grill.

- In a shallow dish, mix the flanken with the soy sauce, sugar, garlic, and black pepper and turn to coat all sides evenly. Allow to sit at room temperature while you make the rice (see page 150) and prepare the sauce.

- To make the sauce, mix the *gochujang* with the *denjang* or miso in a small bowl.

- Heat a grill or grill pan on medium high and make sure it is clean and well oiled before cooking your meat. Remove meat from the marinade and coat with the oil. Season lightly with the salt (the soy sauce will have already seasoned it some) and grill for about 1½ minutes each side. (If you don't have a grill, broil it as close as possible to the heat source.) Wrap in lettuce with some rice and a dab of the *gochujang* mixture and eat.

FOR THE FLANKEN

5½ ounces flanken, bone out, thinly sliced

2 tablespoons soy sauce

2 tablespoons sugar

1 small clove garlic, finely chopped

6 grinds of black pepper

1 tablespoon oil

Salt

FOR THE SAUCE

1 teaspoon *gochujang* (Korean red pepper paste)

1 teaspoon *denjang* or light miso

TO SERVE

1 small head of butter lettuce or romaine

Cooked rice

Skirt Steak with Beets, Poppyseeds, and Crème Fraiche

Remember when skirt steak was just a little more expensive than ground beef and only chefs knew what to do with it? I miss those days. Still, while its price has gone up like a Manhattan apartment, skirt steak is still well marbled, tender, and full flavored, and only takes seconds to cook, so it is perfect for cooking for just yourself as the butchers of yore used to do.

. . . . .

FOR THE BEETS

1 bunch baby beets with tops

2 tablespoons vegetable or other non-flavored oil such as canola

Salt and black pepper

1 large pinch poppyseeds

· Preheat a toaster oven or oven to 400°F. Cut beet tops from the roots and wash both. Reserve the tops. Coat beets with the oil, season with salt and pepper, and bake on a small tray until a small knife can be easily inserted into the thickest part of the largest beet (about 30 minutes for 1-inch-diameter beets).

· In the meantime, prepare the remaining ingredients: Heat a sauté pan on high for a good minute. Add the 2 tablespoons of oil. Season the steak on both sides with salt and pepper, and when the oil is just smoking add the steak. Leave on high heat and cook until browned, about 45 seconds. Flip and cook another 30 seconds or to desired temperature (unfortunately, skirt steak varies in thickness—this amount of time is a good medium rare for a ½-inch-thick piece—adjust timing up or down depending on relative thickness and what temperature you like, but it will taste better if you can caramelize it, hence the high heat), then remove to a warm plate. Pour off any excess oil and reduce heat to medium. Add the onions and the butter and cook until browned and caramelized, stirring to dislodge any bits on the bottom of the pan.

· While the onions cook, mix the crème fraiche with the lemon zest and lemon juice in a small bowl, and season to taste with salt and pepper. If the onions finish browning before the beets are done, remove pan from the heat, but continue stirring occasionally for 2 minutes while the pan loses heat.

· When the beets are done, place them one by one into several layers of paper towel and rub off the skins. Add beets to the pan when finished. Add the poppyseeds and the beet greens and season all with salt and pepper. Stir and place back on the heat. Pour any accumulated juices from the steak back into the pan, cover, and cook just until the greens are wilted. Place over the steak, garnished with the crème fraiche and freshly microplaned or finely grated horseradish to taste.

FOR THE SKIRT STEAK

2 tablespoons vegetable or other non-flavored oil such as canola

One 6-ounce skirt steak, trimmed

1–2 slices onion, halved (about ½ cup)

1 tablespoon butter

TO SERVE

2 tablespoons crème fraiche (substitute sour cream)

1 pinch lemon zest

½ teaspoon lemon juice

Fresh horseradish (optional; or substitute jarred if that's what you have)

Grilled Lamb Shoulder Chop with Fregola, Yogurt, and Mint

······················

People will always let you down. Good food never does. Cry on this shoulder if you must.

· Bring a small pot of water to a boil and add a tablespoon of salt. Dry the lamb chop well and rub with the garlic, cumin, and olive oil. Set aside.

· Boil the fregola in the water until al dente (follow instructions on the package for timing) and drain. Run under cold water until cool. Make sure it is very dry by shaking the excess water from your strainer, then place in a mixing bowl and add the lemon juice, olive oil, grape tomatoes, and red onions and season to taste with salt and pepper.

· Heat a grill pan on high. Oil the grill pan: When very hot, use a paper towel folded several times then doused with a bit of plain oil and wipe down the grates quickly to give them a light coating of oil. This will help the meat to not stick. Season the lamb chop on both sides with salt and pepper and grill until desired temperature. (I like my lamb shoulder medium rare—if it is cut the standard ¾ inch thick, this will take about 2½ minutes per side.) Set aside on a warm place to rest.

· Mix the Greek yogurt with the lemon zest and juice and the garlic and season to taste with salt and pepper. To serve, place the yogurt on a plate, top with the fregola, and garnish with the mint. Serve the lamb on top.

Salt and black pepper to taste

One 8-ounce bone-in lamb shoulder chop

⅔ large clove garlic, finely chopped (use remaining ⅓ below)

½ teaspoon ground cumin

1 tablespoon olive oil, plus more for grill pan

FOR THE FREGOLA

½ cup fregola

1 tablespoon lemon juice

2 tablespoons extra-virgin olive oil

8 grape tomatoes, halved

1 tablespoon red onion, finely sliced

FOR THE YOGURT

3 tablespoons Greek yogurt

1 pinch grated lemon zest

1 teaspoon lemon juice

Remaining ⅓ garlic clove, finely chopped

Salt and black pepper

TO SERVE

3 large leaves mint, sliced

Braised Short Rib with Caramelized Endive

. . . .

Braising is certainly not a quick method of cooking. It takes at least three hours of simmering to break down the collagen and connective tissues in the meat so that it is tender. But often the prep time is minimal, such as in this recipe, and if you start it in the morning in a slow cooker it can be ready by the time you get home from work. Braised meats are even better the next day, so if you make this recipe in bulk, it can be refrigerated or frozen in its braising liquid and eaten for several meals. For this recipe I prefer bone in, with the meat cut into 2 pieces: one approximately 10 ounces and the other 4 ounces for use in Beef and Kimchee Noodle Soup (page 23), which is about 2/3 for the first piece and 1/3 for the second piece. The bone should remain on the larger piece. I like to make the portions from the raw meat, rather than the soft, braised finished dish as it cuts easier. Feel free to increase the amount of meat: the amount here is enough for those two meals. Add a carrot, a rib of celery, and a boiling potato, and you have an old-fashioned pot roast. You'll be rewarded richly.

. . . . .

Don't Waste It!

. . . .

See recipe on page 23 for what to do with
leftover short rib.

· Heat a sauté pan on high. (If not using an electric slow cooker, use your braising pot for sautéing instead.) Season both short rib pieces with salt and pepper on all sides. Add the oil to the pan and swirl, and when smoking, add the meat. Turn heat to medium high and brown on all sides. Remove meat and add the onions, and turn heat to medium. Cook, stirring occasionally, until onions are soft and translucent, about 4 minutes.

· If using a pot, place meat back inside with any juices that have accumulated and cover with chicken stock and add the garlic. Bring to a boil and skim, then turn to a simmer and cook, 3–3½ hours after the boil, adding stock or water as necessary to keep the short rib submerged.

· If using an electric slow cooker, place meat, juices, onion, garlic, and stock in the cooker, cover, set to low, and leave for 8–10 hours. Skim the top of fat, and remove the smaller piece, discarding the bone, plus 2 cups of the resulting broth, and save in a quart container, covered.

· Remove the short rib and add the red wine, bay leaf, and figs. Reduce until well flavored and thickened into a sauce-like consistency. There should be about 3 tablespoons of sauce left. Season to taste, if necessary, with salt and pepper. Replace short rib in the sauce to reheat.

· In the meantime, prepare the endive: Place in a sauté pan, cut side down, with the butter, sugar, and thyme sprig and season with salt. Add ½ inch of water and cook on medium high until water is completely evaporated and the cut sides of the endive are browned throughout. Remove thyme sprig. After plating, top with chives if using. Serve with reheated short rib and figs, topped with the shavings of Parmesan.

FOR THE SHORT RIB

14 ounces short rib, defatted and bone in, cut into 2 pieces: one approximately twice the size of the other, leaving the bone attached to both at the bottom

Salt and black pepper

2 tablespoons vegetable or other non-flavored oil such as canola

½ small onion, sliced (about ⅔ cup)

1 quart chicken stock

1 clove garlic, smashed

½ cup red wine

1 bay leaf

2 or 3 dried figs

FOR THE ENDIVE

1 piece endive, halved lengthwise

1 tablespoon butter

1 teaspoon sugar

1 thyme sprig (optional)

Salt

Pinch chopped chives (optional)

TO SERVE

8 pieces shaved Parmesan cheese (use a peeler)

Korean-Style Pork Spareribs

This Korean American dish takes an hour to bake, but the prep time is minimal. It is sweet, spicy, and sticky, and if you like it enough to have it a second time within a month, double the marinade recipe and store in the refrigerator tightly sealed. It will save you a few minutes the next time. Serve with Tofu Salad (page 163) and a green salad dressed with the same vinaigrette as the tofu.

· · · · ·

3–4 pork spareribs, separated (about 1½ pounds)

Salt and black pepper

2 tablespoons *gochujang* (Korean red pepper sauce)

2 teaspoons rice vinegar

2 tablespoons ketchup

1 teaspoon sesame oil

2 teaspoons sugar

2 teaspoons soy sauce

· Preheat the oven to 400°F. Season the ribs with salt and pepper.

· In a small, shallow baking dish, mix the remaining ingredients. Add the ribs and turn to coat. Wipe down the sides of the dish (otherwise the sugars in the marinade will burn) and cover with tin foil. Bake for 40 minutes, then remove foil and bake another 20 minutes, or until the ribs are nicely glazed and the meat is pulling away from the bones.

CHAPTER 6

SIDES AND BASICS

Crushed
Baby Potatoes

S ometimes being crushed is a good thing, such as with these babies. Smashing them increases the surface area that gets crunchy and caramelized as you pan-roast them. And cooking them twice gives them a soft, creamy interior.

· · · · ·

· Place potatoes in a small pot, cover with cold water seasoned amply with salt, and bring to a boil. Simmer until a knife goes easily into the thickest potato, then drain.

· Heat a small sauté pan on high. Add the oil or fat and, when hot, add the potatoes and smash lightly with a fork. Turn heat to medium high and cook until crisp and browned. Turn and brown the other side. Add the garlic and lemon juice if using and stir to coat all sides. Finish with the herbs if using. Taste; if necessary, add more salt.

⅓ pound baby potatoes such as marble, fingerling, or German butterball

Salt

2 tablespoons oil (olive oil, vegetable oil, duck fat, or bacon fat)

Optional flavoring:
½ clove garlic, finely chopped, and/or a spritz of lemon juice, and/or pinch fresh herbs such as rosemary or thyme

Rice

．．．．．．．．．．．．．．．．．．．．．．．．．．．．．．．．．．．

can remember a time when I didn't know how to cook rice properly. I made watery rice and gooey rice and rice that was still crunchy on top in a very bad way. I was young and hadn't been to cooking school yet and wanted to just wing everything.

Here's what I know now: There's the two-finger method (a two-finger measurement of water above the rice level), there are rice cookers, and then there's this measuring technique, which is more foolproof than the first, and less costly than the second. (You can also do it the way some of the French do and cook rice like pasta, in ample water, draining it when it is tender, but that involves another utensil you have to clean.)

If you think you're going to eat rice again in the next 3–5 days, I'd double this recipe. It reheats very well covered in a microwave. I prefer short grain, but feel free to use long grain—the recipe works for either.

Generally a half a cup of raw rice is a good portion for one person, but feel free to adjust the amount to your appetite and use 1½ times the volume of rice in water.

· Place the rice in a very small, preferably nonstick pot, and rinse several times with cold water, pouring off the water each time.

½ cup rice

· Add ¾ cup of water to the rinsed, drained rice and make sure the rice is level. Place on the stove on high heat. When the water just comes to a boil, stir, cover, and turn heat to its lowest setting. If the rice is bubbling over out of the covered pot, you can try moving it to one side to mitigate the heat. Cook for 20 minutes, then fluff with a fork.

· If you are using most kinds of brown rice, increase the water by 1 tablespoon and cook for 5 minutes longer.

Stir-Fried Greens with Garlic

. . . .•• •....... . . . •••• • .. ... •••

never had a problem eating my vegetables as a child, perhaps because my mother cooked them simply and quickly, the Chinese way, which allows the vegetable's inherent sweetness to come through and lets the greens retain some welcome texture. She used to explain that the darker green the plant was, the better it was for you, and so she saved the leaves that grew around the broccoli plant to cook instead of throwing them away. To this day, I never have a dinner without vegetables, even when no one is watching.

. . . . .

2 tablespoons oil

½ clove garlic, finely chopped

2½ ounces greens such as kale, spinach, bok choy, broccoli rabe, or Swiss chard, sliced if leaves are very large

Salt to taste

· Heat a sauté pan on high. Add the oil and the garlic and when sizzling, add the greens and 2–3 tablespoons of water. Season with salt and cover. Cook until the greens are wilted and the stems are bright green and tender. Taste one with a thicker stem if you are unsure.

NOTE

Try using different oils—you can use olive oil with the addition of a pinch of red pepper flakes added with the garlic for an Italian flavor. Use a non-flavored oil for Asian greens and cut back on some of the salt and replace with a scant tablespoon of oyster sauce, or a teaspoon of *fu yu* (fermented tofu paste).

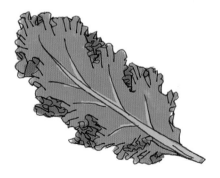

Caramelized Zucchini

love a nice braised zucchini, such as in ratatouille. But a side of zucchini that's basically braising in its own liquids—not so much. Oddly, those sad, spongy, limp ones are produced with the exact same ingredients as the much more delicious ones. All zucchini need is a chunky cut so they don't get overcooked, and some high heat to bring out their natural sugars, for a more complex, caramelized flavor. Feel free to add herbs or other flavorings such as garlic or citrus at the end of the cooking process.

· · · · ·

· Heat a sauté pan on high for a good 2 minutes, until the pan is very hot. Add the olive oil and swirl, then add the zucchini. Season with salt and pepper. Turn heat to medium high and brown, then flip the zucchini over and brown the opposite side.

2 tablespoons olive oil

1 zucchini, about 6–7 inches long, cut in half lengthwise, then cut into 1-inch-thick half moons

Salt and black pepper to taste

Steamed Artichoke with Lemon and Herb Butter

f I'm alone, I like to eat a plain steamed artichoke with melted salted butter. That's all it really needs. Or I'll have it cold with a simple mustard vinaigrette (see recipe page 157), or any kind of pesto. This recipe is a little more complicated than that, but it's endlessly adaptable, and it's delicious, down to the heart.

· Bring a small pot of water to a boil. Add ample salt and the cleaned artichoke. Cover and turn heat to low. Cook until a paring knife is easily inserted into the center of the heart (about 30 minutes).

· In the meantime, melt the butter with the garlic in a small cup on top of the covered pot. Just before serving, stir in the lemon zest and juice and basil, and season to taste with salt and pepper.

1 artichoke, spiny leaf ends snipped off (if necessary), and oxidized stem end removed

3 tablespoons butter

½ clove garlic, pasted

Pinch lemon zest

1 teaspoon lemon juice

1 tablespoon chopped basil (or substitute mint or chives, or 1 teaspoon tarragon)

Salt and black pepper to taste

Arugula Salad with Toasted Pistachios and Parmesan

Charlotte Druckman, my friend and coauthor of my first cookbook, *Cooking Without Borders*, made this salad for me one day out on Long Island, and I've been making it ever since. I love the way the salty richness of the pistachios and Parmesan cheese play against the peppery greens and bracing acidity of the lemon. I think Charlotte cracked the pistachios by hand, but you can also buy them shelled, roasted, and already salted from any drugstore, which saves on time.

· · · · ·

2 ounces arugula (about 1 handful)

1 heaping tablespoon shelled, roasted, salted pistachios

6 shavings of Parmesan cheese (use a peeler), or about 1 ounce or a heaping teaspoon

1 thin slice red onion

1 teaspoon lemon juice

1 tablespoon extra-virgin olive oil

Salt and black pepper to taste

· Mix everything together in a bowl. Taste and adjust seasonings as needed.

Green Salad

et me tell you how I really feel: I find store-bought salad dressings repulsive. They have a chemical aftertaste that stays with you for hours. I get that they are convenient, but they are also an attack on your taste buds, and making your own vinaigrette is a snap. The one below lasts indefinitely in your refrigerator and tastes clean and bright, the way a salad should be. A pinch of herbs will make it even better, but isn't necessary.

. . . . .

· Place the mustard and vinegar in a bowl and whisk until uniform. Slowly drizzle in the oil while whisking to emulsify. Season to taste with salt and pepper and keep the dressing in a jar or sealed plastic container in the fridge for several uses.

· To make the salad (just in case you need guidance on this), place the greens in a bowl and season with a small pinch of salt and a few grinds of pepper, then toss with 2 tablespoons of the dressing and add the herbs if using.

FOR THE MUSTARD
VINAIGRETTE

1 heaping tablespoon Dijon mustard

3 tablespoons red wine vinegar

½ cup extra-virgin olive oil

Salt and black pepper

FOR THE SALAD

2 ounces mesclun

Salt and black pepper

A pinch of fine herbs (equal parts chive, tarragon, parsley, and thyme, optional)

Kale Salad with Dates and Tahini Dressing

There is a little shop in the old Arab quarter in Jerusalem that roasts sesame seeds in an ancient wood-burning oven and then grinds them between two 300-year-old lava rock wheels. They make several kinds, including different roasts and a whole-seed type that has more nutritional value. The results made me want to cook everything with tahini. Basically I had a tahini epiphany—religions of all kinds run strong in Jerusalem.

· Mix everything together. That's it. Then eat it.

2 ounces washed kale, with hard, thick stems removed

Salt and black pepper

3 dates, pitted and roughly chopped

2 tablespoons tahini

1 teaspoon lemon juice

½ small clove garlic, finely chopped

Chickpeas in Tomato

I love chickpeas. They're a little annoying to cook for one person because either you need to have the foresight to soak them the day before if using dried or you're stuck with a partial can of leftovers, but we'll put them to good use. Or, if you can find it, there is a 7-ounce can that works great for one.

·　·　·　·　·

2 tablespoons olive oil

1 slice onion, chopped (about ¼ cup)

½ clove garlic, finely chopped

1 large pinch cumin

1 pinch cayenne pepper

One small ripe tomato, roughly chopped

1 small bay leaf

⅓ of a 15-ounce can chickpeas, rinsed

Salt and black pepper to taste

· In a small pot, heat the olive oil on medium. When shimmering, add the onions and stir. Cook, stirring occasionally, for 3–5 minutes or until soft and translucent but not browned.

· Add the garlic, cumin, and cayenne and stir. Add the tomatoes and bay leaf and stir again. Cook until tomato is reduced and looks like a chunky sauce, about 5–6 minutes. Add the chickpeas and heat through, then add salt and pepper to taste. Remove bay leaf and eat.

Don't Waste It!

You can triple the recipe and eat the other two-thirds for a vegetarian lunch with a nice piece of toasted pita. And leftover chickpeas wouldn't be out of place strewn into Chicken Tagine with Couscous either (page 100).

love whole grains—not because they're good for you (although they are), but because they are chewier and more flavorful and add a nutty complexity that is especially welcome here in this risotto-like dish. Double the recipe and add some greens such as lacinato kale or spinach for a meat-free entrée. Don't worry, I've balanced the farro's virtue by adding some good butter and cheese.

· · · · ·

· In a small pot, melt 1 tablespoon of the butter over medium heat and add the shallot. Stir until soft and translucent, then add the farro and stir.

· Add the white wine and allow to cook off for about a minute, then add the stock. Cover, turn to low, and cook for 25 minutes, or until the grains are soft but not mushy. Stir in the mushrooms and turn heat up to medium high, leaving the pot uncovered. The farro should be a little soupy still. If not, you can add a little more stock. Cook for 2 minutes, then stir in the remaining 1 tablespoon of butter, the thyme, and the lemon zest. Stir in the Parmesan and season to taste with salt and pepper.

2 tablespoons butter

1 tablespoon shallot, minced

⅓ cup farro (or substitute any other kind of wheat berry)

Splash white wine (about 2 tablespoons)

¾–1 cup chicken stock

2 ounces mushrooms such as maitake, shiitake, oyster, or crimini (or wild ones—even better)

A pinch thyme leaves

A pinch microplaned lemon zest

1 heaping tablespoon grated Parmigiano Reggiano cheese

Salt and black pepper to taste

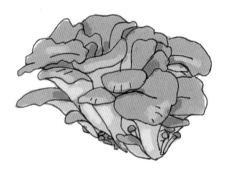

Fennel Salad
with Za'atar

................···..........··**·..··.....

For our very regular customers at annisa who consistently ordered the tasting menu, we liked to do off-menu, on-the-spot creations so they always got something new. We kept a file of these creations so we didn't repeat ourselves. I've often turned to za'atar, a Middle Eastern spice mix made from the eponymous wild herb, plus thyme, toasted sesame seeds, and sumac, to enliven meat, full-flavored fish, or vegetables. As it is already quite a complex flavor, you needn't add too many more ingredients to make a sophisticated, interesting dish.

. . . . .

· Mix all ingredients together. Taste and adjust seasonings.

................··......···....··**·...·......

½ small bulb fennel, browned ends removed, thinly sliced from frond end to root end, then halved lengthwise

A pinch of chopped fronds (optional)

1 thin slice red onion, halved

1 teaspoon lemon juice

1 tablespoon extra-virgin olive oil

½ small clove garlic, finely chopped (optional)

½ teaspoon za'atar spice mix

Salt and black pepper to taste

..........··......···....··**·...·...·..

NOTE

Fennel will oxidize and turn brown if you leave it too long without mixing in the lemon before using.

Tofu Salad

once had a customer who ordered a tasting menu at annisa, but specified that he could only eat white food. No joke. Being a strict hospitalitarian, I rose to the challenge and made one dish of tofu much like the one below, only with white soy sauce, clear organic sesame oil, untoasted sesame seeds, and just the whites of the scallion. Chefs are usually the most neurotic people in the room—but that evening I felt almost normal.

· · · · ·

· Place block of tofu in a shallow bowl and top with the other ingredients.

½ package silken tofu

1 tablespoon soy sauce

1 tablespoon rice wine vinegar

1 tablespoon vegetable or other non-flavored oil such as canola

½ teaspoon sesame oil

Pinch toasted sesame seeds (optional)

1 tablespoon scallion green, sliced

Don't Waste It!

The remaining tofu can be used in place of the eggplant in recipe on page 122.

Broccoli Stem Slaw

Green goddess dressing was popular in the Midwest when I was growing up in the 1970s. Of course, no one made it from scratch—it came in a bottle from a company called Seven Seas and it had a chemical garlic flavor that would stay with you long after you finished your salad. It can't have been good for you. Here is a fresh slaw that makes use of the iconic dressing's essential flavors, is easy to put together, and makes use of ingredients you might throw away—good for your palate, for your health, and for the planet.

· In a small bowl, mash the avocado with the garlic, anchovy paste if using, lemon juice, and olive oil. Stir in the herbs to make a smooth paste. Add the broccoli stems and red onions and season to taste with salt and pepper.

¼ ripe avocado

½ small clove garlic, finely chopped

¼ teaspoon anchovy paste (or to taste, optional)

2 teaspoons lemon juice

2 teaspoons olive oil

1 pinch tarragon leaves, finely chopped

1 large pinch parsley leaves, finely chopped

Stems from 1 bunch broccoli, peeled and julienned with a Japanese mandolin

1 thin slice red onion, chopped (about 2 tablespoons)

Salt and black pepper to taste

Chou au Lardons

This is a classic cold-weather French bistro dish. Lardons are generally hand-cut from slab bacon, but if you can't find that, thick-cut bacon will do. For a quick weeknight dinner, double the recipe and add a boiled sliced potato (put it in the same water you use to cook the cabbage before you bring it to a boil), and place a poached or fried egg on top.

· · · · ·

4–5 ounces green cabbage, core removed, cut into bite-size squares

1 teaspoon oil

1 ounce lardons—thick bacon cut into thick strips

1 slice onion, halved

1 teaspoon red wine vinegar

Salt and black pepper to taste

· Bring a pot of water to a boil and add ample salt, then add cabbage. Bring back to a rolling boil, then drain cabbage and place in a bowl.

· Heat a small sauté pan on high. Add the oil, and when just smoking, add the lardons and turn heat to medium. Allow lardons to brown a little, then turn. You want them to be somewhat rendered, but still chewy—not crunchy. Add the onions and cook until wilted and soft. Remove from the heat and add the vinegar, then pour all over the cabbage. Mix, then season with salt and pepper to taste.

Cauliflower "Giardiniera"

The word *giardiniera* means "gardener" in Italian, and the relish typically contains a mixture of garden vegetables including carrots, peppers, and sometimes gherkins. But my favorite ones in the store-bought jar are the cauliflower florets, so this recipe is my dream version.

· · · · ·

· Mix cauliflower with the salt and 2 cups of water and place in a jar or covered quart container. Shake to dissolve salt, and allow to sit at room temperature overnight.

· The next day, drain and replace in the jar. Add the garlic, oregano, red pepper flakes, and coriander seed to the vinegar and bring to a boil, then pour over the cauliflower. Cover and shake, then refrigerate. The giardiniera is best after it sits a few days.

½ head cauliflower, cut into bite-size pieces

¼ cup salt

1 large clove garlic, smashed

1 pinch oregano

1 large pinch red pepper flakes

½ teaspoon coriander seed

1 pint white vinegar

Don't Waste It!

Making giardiniera is a great way to preserve any leftover cauliflower for use in sandwiches or other recipes such as the bluefish (page 64).

Better
Green Beans

Unless you have a garden or a great greenmarket nearby where you can buy the skinny little French haricots verts, you're usually dealing with green beans that have been picked a long time ago, take a while to cook, and even then still have that spine-chilling tooth squeak that I can't stand. Freshly picked beans take little time to cook to a toothsome tenderness. I've found the best way to deal with beans that have been away from their vines too long is to deep-fry them, the Chinese way. They still maintain some bite while avoiding that Styrofoam-like, nails-on-a-chalkboard result. Toss with a teaspoon of oyster sauce and a pinch of sugar and garlic for something Asian, or chill them in an ice bath and toss with your favorite vinaigrette for a side salad.

NOTE
If using for a salad, just after straining submerge the green beans in ice water to stop the cooking process and keep the bright green color.

· Add 1 inch of oil to a small pot (with high sides—you don't want the oil bubbling over) and heat on medium high until a moistened wooden spoon sizzles immediately when you submerge it. Alternatively, use a thermometer to heat your oil to between 350°F and 375°F.

· Add the beans all at once and cook for 1 minute (or test them at this point to make sure they are tender—if not, keep going for another 30 seconds and check again), then drain into a colander or strainer set over a metal bowl. Season with salt and eat.

Vegetable or other non-flavored oil such as canola

1 cup green beans, ends removed

Salt

Chicken Stock

The most economical way to buy chicken is to purchase it whole and break it down yourself. After removing the breasts and legs, you're still left with a lot of flavor. Making your own chicken stock takes minutes to prep and you're left with something much cleaner and more delicious than anything you can buy. Ever look at the ingredients list on your organic free-range boxed chicken stock? What is "chicken flavor," anyway? And do you need sugar and turmeric in all of the recipes you'll use it in? Just make it yourself. Then you can feed the boiled gizzards and heart to your cat.

· Place chicken parts, onions, celery, and carrots in a pot and add water to cover, then bring to a boil. Skim and turn to a simmer.

· Add remaining ingredients and simmer, skimming occasionally for 2 hours or until well flavored, adding cold water as necessary to keep bones submerged. Turn off heat and allow to sit 30 minutes before straining to allow maximum gelatin to release into the stock.

Bones from 1 chicken plus the gizzards and heart

1 onion, roughly chopped

1 stalk celery, roughly chopped

1 small carrot, roughly chopped

1 large clove garlic, smashed

1 sprig thyme

1 sprig parsley

7 black peppercorns

1 bay leaf

Dashi

ashi is the foundation upon which many Japanese recipes are built. It is a simple stock made from dried kelp (kombu) and bonito flakes—lightly smoked dried and shaved loins of bonito fish, which are a small member of the tuna family.

Bonito flakes also make great cat treats.

· · · · ·

1 small square kombu, about 4 x 4 inches, rinsed

½ cup bonito flakes

· Place the rinsed kombu in a pot and add 1 quart of water. Bring to a boil. Remove from the heat and add the bonito flakes. Allow to steep 15 minutes, then strain through a fine sieve lined with a clean paper towel. Dashi will last chilled and covered in the refrigerator for up to 10 days. Discard if it becomes cloudy or changes color.

Don't Waste It!

See recipes on pages 7, 68, and 104 for what to do with leftover kombu. Simmer the drained bonito in 1 tablespoon mirin and one tablespoon soy sauce with a pinch of sugar, stirring until almost dry. Use as a topping on rice.

Lobster Stock

When I was in cooking school in France, we used fish fumet, or fish bone stock, for any recipe that involved fish, but that was pretty much the last time I saw it used. At my first job at Bouley, the chef used mostly the sweeter, more decadent lobster stock in place of fumet, and I have followed suit. Don't ever throw away your lobster shells. Make stock. Your cat will love the aroma as it cooks.

. . . . .

· Place the lobster shells and head in a pot with the vegetables. Cover with cold water and bring to a boil. Skim and turn to a simmer.

· Add remaining ingredients and simmer, skimming occasionally, for 1–1½ hours or until well flavored. Add more water as necessary during cooking to keep ingredients submerged. Strain.

Shell and head of one lobster

1 small onion, roughly chopped

1 large clove garlic, smashed

1 small carrot, roughly chopped

1 celery stalk, roughly chopped

1 tomato, roughly chopped (optional)

1 sprig thyme

1 sprig tarragon

1 sprig parsley

1 bay leaf

7 peppercorns

CHAPTER 7

SWEETS

Grapefruit with Elderflower and Mint

G rapefruit and elderflower are a common pairing in cocktails, which is where the idea for this super-fast, super-refreshing dessert comes from. Hell, throw in some gin or vodka as well and have a little solo party.

· · · · ·

· Section the grapefruit either by peeling it and then peeling off the outer membrane of each segment, or by cutting off both the stem and flower ends, then cutting off the peel strip by strip, starting from one open/cut-off end and ending at the other in an arc-shaped movement, cutting just down to the flesh.

· Once you have a globe of the red inner flesh, run your knife along either side of the sections, just next to the membrane, to release skinless segments. Remove seeds as you go. Mix with the elderflower and top with the mint and enjoy.

1 small red grapefruit (or half a larger grapefruit)

1 tablespoon elderflower syrup or St-Germain liqueur

2 large mint leaves, sliced

Strawberries with Aged Balsamic Vinegar and Mascarpone

........·..··..·............··.·....·..·...

Aged balsamic vinegar, while pricey, can transform a piece of good fruit or a mild, creamy cheese into a stunning dessert. You need to get real balsamic from Emilia-Romagna (it won't be found in an average grocery store), aged for at least twelve years. The older the better and more complex; the vinegar becomes more concentrated and picks up the flavors of the barrels it is aged in over the years. A small bottle of thirty-year-old vinegar can cost close to $100, but you don't need much—and aren't you worth it?

· Mix the sliced strawberries with the 2 teaspoons of sugar, ½ teaspoon of the lemon juice, and black pepper.

· In another small bowl mix the mascarpone with the 2 tablespoons of sugar and remaining lemon juice, plus the lemon zest and salt. Top with the strawberries and drizzle with the balsamic vinegar.

½ cup sliced strawberries

2 tablespoons plus 2 teaspoons sugar

1½ teaspoons lemon juice

A grinding of black pepper

⅓ cup mascarpone cheese

A few gratings of lemon zest on a microplane

Pinch salt

1 teaspoon aged balsamic vinegar (substitute ⅓ cup regular balsamic reduced in a small pan to a glaze)

The Only Crumble Topping Recipe You'll Ever Need When Baking for Yourself

Here is another recipe that you can use in many different applications. The next four recipes use a quarter of this base, and the rest can be kept in the refrigerator in a covered container for up to two weeks or in the freezer for a month. If you use a vacuum sealer and portion it in useable amounts, it can last indefinitely—but I think you'll like it so much that it won't last very long.

. . . . .

1 cup flour

½ cup light brown sugar

2 tablespoons granulated sugar

8 tablespoons butter

Pinch salt

Pinch cinnamon

¼ cup regular oats

· Place the flour, sugars, butter, salt, cinnamon, and oats in a bowl. Using your fingers, mix together until lumps form.

· Chill at least 20 minutes before using. Refrigerate or freeze in useable portions whatever you don't use immediately, covered tightly for another use.

Fruit Crumble

I n the summertime, I like to keep my crumble topping on hand to make a quick, easy pie-like dessert out of any ripe (or overripe) fruit I have on hand. As it bakes, the top gets crunchy, and the bottom that is in contact with the fruit soaks up a little of the juices so you have a textural segue of a delicious sort. It's a good idea to taste your fruit before baking and adjust the sugar content accordingly. If you're using a piece of rhubarb, for example, you'll want to increase the sugar content, as rhubarb is really tart with little natural sugar. But if you have amazingly sweet berries, perhaps you'll use less. Of course, a scoop of vanilla ice cream on top never hurts.

· · · · ·

· Preheat oven to 400°F.

· Mix the fruit, sugar, salt, lemon juice, and cornstarch or tapioca starch in a small bowl. Place in a mini pie pan and top with the crumble mixture. Place in the preheated oven and bake about 25 minutes, until the top is browned and crisp and the fruit is bubbling.

½ cup fruit, cut into 1-inch pieces if larger than that

1 tablespoon plus 2 teaspoons granulated sugar (or to taste)

Pinch salt

1 teaspoon lemon juice

1 teaspoon cornstarch or tapioca starch

¼ crumble recipe (recipe page 180)

Peanut Butter and Chocolate Pie

．．．．．．．．．．．．．．．．．．．．．．．．．．．

There was a booth at one of the many food festivals I participate in every year that claimed to be able to tell what kind of person you were based on your candy choices. It was a ridiculous premise, but part of me wanted to believe the outcome—that because I chose crunchy candies such as malted milk balls I was somehow adventurous, inquisitive, and always up for a surprise. I'd think the same would be true for peanut butter choices. Crunchy and smooth both work here. So what's it going to be? This could be a life-changing choice.

· Preheat your oven or toaster oven to 375°F. Coat a 4-inch mini pie mold with cooking spray or butter (you can use a heatproof ramekin, but the cooking time may be a little longer). Cut a circle of parchment paper that's an inch or two bigger than your mold. Using the palm of your hand, press the crumble mixture into an even layer in a circle slightly larger than your mold but smaller than the paper so that the dough will cover the bottom and sides of the tin. You can take a little dough from another area to make a patch if needed. Flip and gently press into the prepared mold. Add some dried beans or another mini pie tin to weigh it down. If using another pie tin, cook the crust upside down. This is to help the crumble mixture hold the shape of the mold and is called "blind baking" (not sure why—make your own postulations). Bake for 20 minutes or until crispy and golden brown throughout. Remove parchment paper and set aside on a rack to cool.

· In the meantime, make the peanut butter filling: Mix the peanut butter with the cream, sugar, and vanilla extract. Add to the baked and cooled pie crust and top with the chopped chocolate.

Cooking spray or butter

¼ cup crumble topping (recipe page 180)

¼ cup peanut butter

1 tablespoon cream

1 tablespoon plus 2 teaspoons light brown sugar

Dash vanilla extract

1½ ounces chocolate, chopped (optional)

Salted Butterscotch Pie

My mother always had a jar of butterscotch candies on her desk at the hospital where she was a pathologist. It was the one thing my siblings and I looked forward to as kids when we'd visit. The buttery caramel was a welcome antidote to the smell of hospital sanitizer that pervaded every room. The warm, soft brown color of the treats were a respite from her lab's harsh fluorescent lights, and the sweetness a comfort during what was sometimes a scary experience. To this day, I gravitate toward any butterscotch dessert, and I usually have something on my menu at annisa in that vein. In any form, it is always a nostalgic flavor— forever reassuring.

· Preheat your toaster oven to 375°F. Coat a 4-inch mini pie mold with some cooking spray or butter (you can use a heatproof ramekin, but the cooking time may be a little longer). Cut a circle of parchment paper that's an inch or two bigger than your mold. Using the palm of your hand, press the crumble mixture into an even layer in a circle slightly larger than your mold but smaller than the paper so that the dough will cover the bottom and sides of the tin. You can take a little from another area to make a patch if needed. Flip and gently press into the prepared mold. Remove paper.

· Mix the mascarpone, the pinch of sugar, and the egg white together until smooth, then transfer into the pie shell. Bake for 20 minutes or until mascarpone is set and the crust is browned. Set aside on a rack to cool.

· In the meantime, make the butterscotch. Place the brown sugar, butter, small pinch of regular salt, and corn syrup in a small pot and bring to a boil on medium-high heat. Stir once and cook until syrupy, about 1 minute or less—do not overcook or your butterscotch will be too chewy (although still tasty). Stir in the cream and take off the heat. Allow to cool slightly, then pour into the baked, cooled pie crust and chill. Sprinkle with a bit of Maldon salt or other unflavored finishing salt and enjoy.

Cooking spray or butter

¼ cup crumble topping (recipe page 180)

3 tablespoons mascarpone

1 pinch granulated sugar

1 tablespoon egg white

2 tablespoons plus 2 teaspoons light brown sugar

1 teaspoon butter

1 small pinch salt

1 tablespoon corn syrup

2 teaspoons heavy cream

Pinch Maldon salt

Don't Waste It!

See recipe for Meyer Lemon Curd Pie (page 186) for what to do with leftover egg.

Meyer Lemon Curd Pie

I f life gives you lemons, there are endless ways of preparing them. If life gives you Meyer lemons, celebrate! Sunny and yellow, with bright, juicy flesh and fragrant, floral zest, Meyer lemons are the ultimate optimistic fruit. They bring excitement and a complex cheer to any dish that calls for regular lemon, such as in this *tarte au citron*, or lemon pie. My regular grocery store carries them now, so hopefully you won't have difficulty finding them. If you do, try a specialty grocer, or substitute a regular lemon, but halve the amount of zest.

· Preheat your toaster oven or oven to 375°F. Coat your 4-inch mini pie mold with cooking spray or butter (you can use a heatproof ramekin, but the cooking time may be a little longer). Cut a circle of parchment paper that's an inch or two bigger than your mold. Using the palm of your hand, press the crumble mixture into an even layer in a circle slightly larger than your mold but smaller than the paper, so that the dough will cover the bottom and sides of the tin. You can take a little from another area to make a patch if needed. Flip and gently press into the prepared mold. Add some dried beans or another mini pie tin to weigh it down. If using a pie tin, cook the crust upside down. This is to help the crumble mixture hold the shape of the mold. Bake for 20 minutes or until crispy and golden brown throughout. Remove parchment paper and set aside on a rack to cool.

· Bring a small pot of water to a boil, then turn it to a simmer. Mix the yolk, lemon juice and zest, and sugar together in a metal bowl that is large enough to sit in the pot of water without overturning. Place bowl over the pot and whisk for 5 minutes or until the mixture starts to thicken. Add the butter and the pinch of salt and continue whisking until incorporated. Remove and chill, then fill the baked pie crust with the curd.

Cooking spray or butter

¼ cup crumble recipe (recipe page 180)

1 poorly separated yolk (leave a little white attached)

2 tablespoons Meyer lemon juice (about 1 lemon)

Zest of 1 Meyer lemon

¼ cup sugar

2 ounces butter (4 tablespoons)

Pinch salt

Orange
Olive Oil Cake

s it your birthday? Don't buy a cupcake. Make yourself this special confection, which takes less than ten minutes to whip up and tastes like a warm holiday on the Mediterranean. There are people out there that get married to themselves ... in public. So hell, put a candle in it and make a wish.

· · · · ·

¼ cup flour

3 tablespoons sugar

1 medium egg white, beaten

1 good pinch salt

3 tablespoons olive oil

2 tablespoons milk

1 teaspoon lemon juice

1 large pinch microplaned zest of orange (no white pith)

· Mix the flour and sugar together in a ramekin or Pyrex pint container.

· In another bowl, beat the egg white with the salt and add the olive oil, milk, lemon juice, and orange zest. Add to the flour mixture and stir with a fork until smooth. Microwave on high for 2 minutes.

Sesame "Ice Cream"

This isn't really an ice cream per se, more an iced cream. It has the texture of a semifreddo, the Italian frozen dessert that is usually made with cooked eggs before freezing. My version tastes like a creamy halva—Middle Eastern sesame candy—and is a cinch to make. I whip the cream to make the end result softer, but you could skip that step for a more icy texture reminiscent of actual halva.

· · · · ·

· Make sure your cream is cold. If it is particularly hot where you are cooking, place cream in a bowl nestled in another bigger bowl filled with ice.

· Add the sugar and salt and whip with a wire whisk to just form hard peaks—when you dip the whisk into the cream and lift up, the resulting peak of cream should not fall over. Gently fold in the tahini and freeze, covered, until set.

1/3 cup heavy cream

2 tablespoons sugar

Good pinch of salt

2 tablespoons tahini

Caramelized
Banana with
Coconut

The banana is a loaded fruit. Kids find the name hysterical (note the popular Minions movies: "BA NA NA!"). Early comedy relied on the image of a person slipping on its peel. Fishermen won't allow bananas aboard boats, believing them to be bad luck. Many Asian Americans such as myself identify with its yellow on the outside and white on the inside appearance. And, of course, there's its phallic symbolism. But never mind all that! Bananas are delicious topped with crunchy caramel and served with another tropical ingredient, coconut. What grows together, goes together, as they say.

· If you have a blowtorch, see instructions below. If not, preheat your broiler on high. Lay the banana cut sides up on a heatproof dish and coat the cut sides with roughly 1 tablespoon of sugar each in an even, thick-ish layer about 1/16–1/8 inch thick. Place under the broiler as close as possible to the heat source and watch closely until the sugar bubbles all over and caramelizes.

· Alternatively, use a blowtorch to the same effect. Point flame directly at the sugar, not getting so close that all the sugar gets blown off, but not so far away that it doesn't cook. As the sugar bubbles and caramelizes, move down the banana until all the sugar has been cooked. No sugar crystals should remain, and the cut sides of the banana should be single glossy layers of dark brown caramel. A little burning may occur, but don't worry unless it's completely scorched.

· Bring the coconut milk, the remaining 2 tablespoons of the sugar, and the pinch of salt to a rolling boil in a small pot or sauté pan. Allow to cool (still a little warm is okay) and serve as a sauce over the caramelized banana.

1 small banana, peeled and split lengthwise

4 tablespoons granulated sugar, plus an extra pinch for sprinkling

1/3 cup coconut milk

Pinch salt

Chocolate
Pain Perdue

....

ere is a great use for old bread. *Pain perdue* (pronounced "peh pare-*doo*") is just a fancy name for French toast and has nothing to do with physical hurt or industrialized chickens. It means "lost bread," which is somewhat of a misnomer; with its bath of custard and its gilding of brown butter, this bread is anything but lost.

· Mix the sugar, cocoa powder, and salt in a shallow dish and slowly whisk in the milk and egg yolk. Add the bread and coat on all sides, allowing it time to soak up as much of the custard mixture as possible.

· Melt the butter in a sauté pan on medium high and swirl to coat. Add the bread, cut side down, and press lightly with a spatula to ensure full contact with the pan. Allow to brown (you'll have to watch closely—this shouldn't take more than 2 minutes), then flip and top with the chopped chocolate. Brown the other side. The chopped chocolate should melt. Top with the nuts if using and eat.

· · · · ·

1 tablespoon plus 2 teaspoons sugar

2 teaspoons cocoa powder

1 pinch salt

⅓ cup milk

1 egg yolk

3-inch length of plain baguette or a similar quantity of other plain, day-or-more-old bread, halved lengthwise

2 tablespoons butter

1½ ounces semisweet or other eating chocolate, chopped

1 tablespoon chopped roasted nuts such as almonds, walnuts, pecans, or pistachios (optional)

Don't Waste It!

See recipe for Orange Olive Oil Cake (page 188) for what to do with the egg white.

Panna Cotta

T his Italian-style milk-based pudding takes a little time to set, but if you make it before your dinner and put it in a shallow bowl, it should be done by the time you're ready for dessert. If you want it faster, nestle the bowl in a bigger bowl of ice water before placing in the refrigerator. And feel free to play around with the recipe—the vanilla flavoring can be replaced with endless variations such as saffron, almond, or cinnamon, as can the toppings. Even the milk and cream can be replaced—try yogurt, crème fraiche, or your favorite nut or soy milk. But you'll want some sort of milk product in order for it to still be panna cotta, which means "cooked milk" in Italian.

· Mix the gelatin with 2 teaspoons of water and allow to bloom while you prepare the remaining ingredients.

· Mix the milk, cream, sugar, and salt in a small pot and halve the vanilla bean lengthwise. Scrape the seeds from within and add to the pot along with the deseeded pod. Bring to a boil. Remove from the heat and stir in the gelatin mixture, which should, at this point, be translucent and have formed a rubbery mass. Strain into a small bowl and refrigerate until set, about an hour or so. If you can't wait to eat it, place the entire bowl in an ice bath to speed the process. Top with one of the suggested toppings if using and eat.

1 teaspoon gelatin

½ cup milk

¼ cup cream

2 tablespoons plus 1 teaspoon sugar

1 pinch salt

1 inch of a vanilla bean pod (substitute a smidgen of vanilla paste)

Suggested toppings (optional): a heaping tablespoon of good jam, ¼ cup fresh or macerated fruit, 1 tablespoon candied fruit rind (such as grapefruit or orange), a sprinkling of chopped nuts

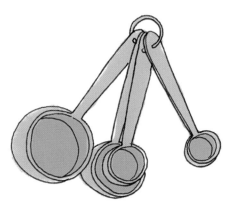

Concord Grape Soup with Crème Fraiche

· · · · · ·· ··· ··· ···· ···

I n the fall, the smell of Concord grapes is everywhere on Long Island. They grow wild and rampant, and if you follow your nose and look above you and around you, you'll find the potent orbs dangling from vines clinging to trees, bushes, and fences. In no time you can harvest a free bushel. Eating them is another story. It's a messy labor of love, with thick skins you'll want to suck dry before discarding, and plentiful, astringent seeds to eat around. You'll be left with purple hands and lips, and a contented sigh. If you plan on going out later, however, this soup will leave you more presentable, and is perhaps faster and easier than eating a bowlful of grapes plain.

· · · · ·

1 cup Concord grapes, stems off, green ones discarded

1 tablespoon sugar, or to taste

Pinch salt

1 dollop crème fraiche

· Place the grapes, sugar, and salt in the chopper attachment that came with your hand blender and puree. Strain. Taste and adjust seasonings and serve in a bowl, chilled, with a dollop of crème fraiche.

Pineapple Times Three: Roasted, Frozen, and in a Glass

····· ··· ···················· ··· ··· ···

They actually grow mini pineapples that are suitable for one. If you can find one in your specialty grocery store, you're golden. If not, you can sometimes find pre-cut pineapple pieces that will do—or you can just go all out and get a big one. In that case, I have included two other pineapple recipes so none will go to waste (if you don't end up eating it all in its natural state). The last recipe is classic South American, and is a brilliant use of the parts you'd normally discard.

If you happen to locate the mini pineapple and would like to use up the by-product, cut the recipe down by four. You can even plant the green top after it has been lopped off—keep it indoors if you don't live in a tropical climate. In a few years, you might have another pineapple to harvest.

· Preheat oven or toaster oven to 375°F. Line a baking tray with parchment paper to ease the cleanup process.

· Place pineapple on baking tray, cover evenly with the sugar, and season evenly with the salt. Dot with the butter and bake for 25–30 minutes or until the edges start to turn dark brown and caramelize.

· · · · · · · · ·• • • ·• • • • • • • • • • • • • • • •• •• ·• •• •• •• •• • • •

ROASTED

1 plank of cored pineapple (or equivalent) (about 2 x 6 x ½ inch)

1 heaping tablespoon light brown sugar

Pinch salt

1 tablespoon butter

· Puree all ingredients in a blender, place in a container, cover, and freeze. Break up with a fork before eating.

PINEAPPLE GRANITA

Cored and peeled pineapple meat

Sugar to taste (about 1 tablespoon per cup of puree)

Pinch salt

· Place all ingredients in a pot and bring to a boil. Turn to a simmer and cook until well flavored, about 15–20 minutes. Strain and chill.

PINEAPPLE CINNAMON DRINK

Pineapple peelings and core

1 stick cinnamon

2 quarts water

¾ cup sugar (or to taste)

1 tablespoon lemon juice (or to taste)

· · · · · · ·•• •• • • • • • • • • • • • • •• • •• •• ·• • • • •

INGREDIENTS

My cooking school instructors in France always said that shopping was 50 percent of the effort in creating a dish. That is, if you purchased good ingredients, you're already halfway there. The chef David Chang, of Momofuku bar fame, joked that in California, it's 75 percent of the effort—intimating that the chefs there don't do much cooking. Either way, here is a guide for shopping for one.

WHERE TO SHOP

When buying single-portion-size ingredients, it is sometimes best to steer clear of your generic grocery store. Specialty markets such as fishmongers and butchers can sell you exactly what you need instead of prepackaged items more suitable for feeding an entire family. Your local farmer's market is also a good place to start. This may take a little more travel time, but if you're organized and plan out the week's menu in advance, you can minimize your visits. And if this isn't possible, see "Cold Storage Tips" (page 212) and "Organizing Your Freezer" (page 217).

STOCK UP

The key to cooking for one multiculturally with ease is to have an arsenal of dry goods always on hand. While American grocery stores are stocking more and more international ingredients (my local Gristedes now has Korean *gochujang* and *denjang*, and my King Kullen on Long Island carries bean thread noodles and kimchee), it can still take too much time to visit multiple stores to find what you want. Whole Foods and your local health food store are good places to look for more esoteric items, but if you live in a place that has none of these, I suggest taking a few minutes to stock your pantry by ordering it all on the internet in one fell swoop (almost everything is available online). Generally, when buying Chinese ingredients, choose a Chinese brand (La Choy is not a Chinese brand, fyi), when buying Japanese, choose a Japanese brand, and so on. Dry goods can last indefinitely, so you'll have them on hand for many meals to come.

WHAT TO BUY AS BASICS

I like to always have some basics on hand. This makes shopping simpler, and you can always cull a last-minute, balanced meal from these items without even having to stop at a store. The following is my suggested bare-minimum list. The more often you cook at home, the larger the quantity you should have on hand, and the longer this list can be. The more the merrier on the dry goods.

DRY GOODS	GROCERY
Non-flavored cooking oil such as vegetable or canola	Onions
Olive oil	Garlic
Finishing olive oil (higher quality)	Lemons
Smooth mustard	Carrots
Bay leaves	Eggs
Cayenne	Potatoes (waxy such as red-skinned and Idaho)
Cinnamon	Red onion
Japanese soy sauce	Milk
Red wine vinegar	Salad greens (or the vegetable you eat most)
Rice wine vinegar	Butter
Balsamic vinegar	Oranges
Fish sauce	Tomatoes
Pasta (various shapes such as spaghetti and penne)	
Canned tomatoes	
Olives (various: Kalamata, Niçoise, and a green type)	KEEP FROZEN
White wine	Leftover jalapeños
Red wine	Thai bird chilies
Capers	Lemongrass
Anchovies	Kaffir lime leaf
Clam juice	
Chicken stock	
All-purpose flour	
Kosher or sea salt	
Black pepper	
Granulated sugar	
Brown sugar	
Tabasco	
Sriracha	
Asian sesame oil	
Pistachios or some other nuts	
Cumin, ground	
Coriander seed, ground	

Bonito flakes

Lightly smoked, dried, and shaved loins of bonito, a member
of the tuna family. An essential ingredient in Japanese
cuisine used to make the soup stock dashi, and to garnish
dishes.

Calabrian chilies

Calabrian chilies are fruity, spicy red chilies grown in
Calabria, Italy. I like the Tutto Calabria brand. Get the crushed
ones (not the dried ones) in a jar to save on chopping time.
They're great on pizza, pasta, in stews, and in salads.

Chaat masala

A blend of spices containing mango powder, cumin, chili
powder, ginger powder, black salt, asafetida, and sugar.
Available at www.kalustyans.com.

Chinese fermented black beans

Also known as *dou chi*. These are the salted, fermented,
and semi-dried black soybeans that are the key ingredient
in black bean sauce. My mother always kept them in the
cupboard at room temperature, but for some reason I keep
them in an airtight container in the refrigerator. In any case,
they have a very long shelf life.

Chinese five-spice powder

A spice blend of cinnamon, star anise, fennel, Szechuan
peppercorn, and cloves. Available in Asian markets or online.

Chinese sausage

Also known as *lap cheong*. This fatty, sweet, dried pork sausage is used in Cantonese cooking.

Dang myun

Korean noodles made from yam starch. An essential ingredient in *jap chae*. Order them online at www.hmart.com or substitute glass noodles if you must.

Denjang

Korean miso paste. Substitute Japanese light miso.

Dried anchovies

Also known as iriko, these little dried fish add depth and umami to northern Asian stews. They can also be lightly fried and eaten as a snack.

Dried kombu

Dried kelp, which is an essential ingredient in Japanese cooking. It is high in amino acids and thus umami. It is used to make dashi, and can be eaten on its own, fried, plain, or braised.

Dried shrimp

This Chinese product comes in different sizes but is essentially dried krill used to flavor dishes. I generally use the smaller ones that are a centimeter long or less as I simply chop them before using.

Fennel pollen

This is a harder-to-find, chef-y ingredient that will really blow your mind once you have it in your possession. Unless you live in a big city, you'll probably need to order it online. It has a powerful, slightly sweet, and funky flavor that is a key ingredient in Italian porchetta and would be lovely sprinkled on panna cotta (see recipe page 194) or yogurt.

Fish sauce

A brown, salty, umami-rich fluid made from salted, fermented anchovies. Commonly used in Southeast Asia.

Garam masala

A spice mix used in South Asian cooking. The blends vary from region to region, but generally the Indian ones are made from peppercorns, bay leaf, cumin, cloves, cardamom, mace, and nutmeg. Available at www.kalustyans.com.

Glass noodles

Also known as bean thread noodles, or cellophane noodles. They are made from mung bean starch and are widely used in Asia. Buy the ones that are separated into single-portion packages, otherwise they are difficult to pull apart.

Gochujang

Korean fermented chili and soybean paste. Keep refrigerated after opening.

Harissa

A North African chili paste generally made from various red chilies, garlic, coriander, cumin, mint, and olive oil. There are different versions of this condiment, but I generally like to buy those in a jar or a tube as they keep longer. Otherwise you can freeze it.

Kaffir lime leaf

These are the fragrant leaves of the kaffir lime tree, used in Thai cuisine. Buy them fresh and then keep them in the freezer in a ziplock or FoodSaver bag.

Kimchee

There are many kinds of kimchee made from various vegetables with regional differences in Korea. The most ubiquitous is made from Napa cabbage that is salted and mixed with Korean ground chilies, garlic, garlic chives, scallions, onions, fish sauce, and sometimes oysters or fermented shrimp, then fermented. No Korean meal is complete without kimchee. Available at www.hmart.com.

Korean ground chili

Also known as *gochu garu*. This is a bright red ground chili from Korea that is sweet and mildly spicy. It comes both finely and more coarsely ground. I usually use the coarsely ground one. Available at www.hmart.com.

Lao Gan Ma

Also known as "Old Godmother Sauce." This company makes several chili condiments, but the one you want is the one with the unhappy Chinese woman on the label. I'd be unhappy too if someone put my face on a jar labeled "Old Godmother," but I'm always happy to eat this. Use it on noodles, meats, tofu, and eggs. It has a Szechuan flavor and is crunchy, too. (I know this is akin to saying something has a "New England flavor," but what I mean is that it has that tingly, spicy, garlicky, fermented flavor typical of much of Szechuan's most famous dishes.)

Lemongrass

This lemony, astringent, and somewhat floral grass is used as a flavoring in Southeast Asian cuisines. Remove the dry outer leaves before using, and pound it to maximize the release of flavor. It can be frozen.

Masa harina

Cornmeal made from Mexican lime-slaked corn. Available in some grocery stores, Latin grocery stores, and online.

Meyer lemon

Meyer lemons are darker yellow and usually a little softer than regular lemons. They are also more fragrant and floral. Some say they are a cross between a regular lemon and a tangerine, and some say that they were brought to California from China by a guy named Meyer. In any case, they are one of my favorite flavors. Look for them in your local specialty grocery store.

Mirin

Naturally sweet rice wine, low in alcohol and widely used in Japanese cuisine. Store at room temperature and wipe the bottle clean after each use to prevent bug attraction.

Olive oil

Don't fall for the more rustic-sounding, unfiltered types—the residue makes olive oil go off much faster. Olive oil should be stored in a cool, dark place, and should come either in a dark green bottle or a tin, as light (and heat) will turn it rancid. It loses its flavor when you heat it, so I like to have two or three levels of olive oil around. I like an inexpensive one for cooking (I'll still buy extra-virgin, or the first cold pressing, although it's not necessary for this use, as once you heat it to temperatures typical for sautéing the flavor disappears). I like a middle range of olive oil to use for dressings—for this I use an organic Chilean brand, Olave. For finishing, you need to spend some money. I like Castillo de Canena from Spain. You can go crazy at this point, as there are many kinds made from many different olives that produce a wide range of styles and flavors, but the one made from arbequina olives is versatile and amazing. Whatever you decide on, be sure to get the latest harvest. Available at www.oliveoillovers.com.

Oyster sauce

Oyster sauce is a Chinese condiment used all over Southeast Asia. It is made with sugar, salt, cornstarch, and oyster extract, and adds a deep, rich flavor to sauces. I sometimes use a little of it to augment the flavor of shellfish stews if the seafood flavor isn't potent enough. I like the Lee Kum Kee and Panda brands.

Rice noodles

Most grocery stores have this in their Asian section these days, but there are many different kinds, from vermicelli to wide flat ones. They are mostly interchangeable, although each lends a different texture to whatever you are making.

Salt

I like to use kosher salt, which is inexpensive and pure. Plain, fine sea salt is even better, but costlier. In these recipes I call for salt to taste, as people like different salt levels. But if you're wondering why restaurant food tastes so much better than what you make at home, it's almost certainly the heavier seasoning. When you're making a dish, make sure each element is seasoned individually. It is not enough, for example, to season just the meat that goes into a stew without seasoning the vegetables and the finished braising liquid as well.

S&B Curry Powder

This is an East Asian brand of curry powder, but you can substitute madras powder.

Shishito peppers

I love these sweet green peppers that are occasionally a little spicy (one out of ten, they say), even though I have a strong aversion to green bell peppers. I find shishitos at my local greenmarket in the summertime, or at specialty grocers. They are very similar to Spanish padron peppers, which can be used interchangeably. If you can't find either of those, try using banana peppers or long hot green chilies. And if you can't find *those*, use a red or orange bell pepper. Shishitos are available online, but not in quantities suitable for one, and I don't suggest freezing them.

Soba

Japanese buckwheat flour noodles, available in the Asian section of most grocery stores these days.

Star anise

This dried spice is used in Chinese and Vietnamese braises and comes from the fruit of an evergreen tree native to southern Asia.

Thai basil

This basil has purple stems and skinnier leaves than Italian basil and has an anise-like flavor. Available fresh at www.ImportFood.com.

Thai bird chilies

Also known as "bird's-eye chilies," these small red or green chilies pack a punch. Be careful with them—one of my male cooks once made the mistake of chopping a bunch of them without wearing gloves, then visiting the bathroom . . .

Tuong Ot Toi Vietnam

Vietnamese chili-garlic sauce. This used to be available only in specialty stores but is now widely available.

Za'atar

A Middle Eastern spice mix generally made with the za'atar herb, which is like a wild oregano, plus sumac, salt, sesame seeds, and thyme.

COLD STORAGE TIPS

....

Here are some guidelines to help maximize the shelf life of your ingredients.

Fruits and vegetables

For the most part, fruits and vegetables will stay fresh longer in your refrigerator if you keep them in a plastic bag in the crisper. This includes longer-lasting items such as potatoes and citrus. Onions and garlic bulbs do not need a plastic bag until they are cut into or broken open; then a ziplock bag will help them keep longer. If using only part of an onion that you won't be using again soon, leave the papery peel on the remaining part to help keep it from drying out.

Fruits and vegetables that are best kept at room temperature are tomatoes (the texture will change for the worse upon refrigeration), avocadoes, large stone fruits, pears (until they are ripe), and bananas (until they are ripe—once ripe, they must be kept in a plastic bag if you are to refrigerate them or the skins will blacken). Other fruits are fine at room temperature if you like them that way.

Generally, mushrooms should not be kept in plastic or they will sweat, and the water ruins them. This is not as big of an issue for closed-cap cultivars such as button or cremini. For others, keep in a brown paper bag, or in a container covered with a dry cloth or paper towel.

Ginger

The best way to keep ginger is on top of the soil of a houseplant. It may even grow that way. Cut off the dry ends farthest from the growth when using.

Herbs

If you aren't going to bother growing your own herbs, they should be kept in the fridge in sealed ziplock bags with dry paper towels wrapped around them.

Seafood

It is best to use seafood the day you purchase it. But if you need to store it, place an ice pack or a ziplock bag filled with ice on top of it in the refrigerator and use within two to three days. Or freeze, preferably in a vacuum-sealed bag. Cover shellfish with a wet rag in a bowl before topping with an ice pack. Do not leave submerged in water, or the flavor will leach out and the shellfish will die.

Meat

Red meat doesn't like light, so keep it wrapped in the butcher paper or plastic that it came in. Once opened, if you are to use it again in the next few days, wrap tightly in parchment paper, securing with tape to store.

Cheese

Most aged cheeses are alive and are, for the most part, best if not suffocated. Keep them in the paper they came in. This isn't the case for fresh cheeses like mozzarella (which is best as soon as it is made anyway). Keep it wrapped as tightly as possible with as little air contact as possible. Feta also doesn't like air. Cut the cheese so the remainder can stay submerged in the brine in which it came. Parmesan can be vacuum sealed, as it dries out easily.

Nuts and whole grains

Keep these in the refrigerator in airtight containers. That's right—in the fridge, not the pantry. The oils in both of these items go rancid easily, but refrigerating them will deter that process.

SUGGESTED
EQUIPMENT

· · · · · · · ·:· ·:· ·...· · · · ·.·· · ·...·..· · ·

Aside from a stove, a cutting board, a few knives, a few pots, pans, and mixing bowls, and some utensils, these items can help ease preparation and help with storage and cleanup when cooking for one.

Immersion blender with chopper attachment
Use to make small amounts of purees and compound butters, emulsify sauces, and more. A traditional blender needs larger volumes of ingredients in order for the blades to be immersed and therefore function properly.

FoodSaver vacuum sealer and bags
This is a brilliant piece of equipment that sucks the air out of the storage bag and seals ingredients in so they are far less likely to develop freezer burn. You can also use just the sealer mode without suction to reseal pretty much anything that comes in a plastic-y bag, such as chips. It's great for brown sugar, so you don't get that unusable-brown-brick effect.

1-quart nonstick saucepot
I use this for making rice. The nonstick surface makes it so much easier to clean, and it can be used for any other small cooking tasks as well.

1½-quart clay pot
This isn't necessary, but you can cook and eat from it and still feel civilized while eliminating one more item to clean.

Toaster oven

Nothing beats a real oven for consistent and accurate heat retention, but for small tasks this piece of equipment shouldn't be overlooked. And they're making much nicer ones these days with convection capabilities. When I went to cooking school in Paris, I lived in a tiny studio in the Marais that basically had its kitchen on the wall of the entry hallway. It had a three-foot-high refrigerator with two or three hot plates on top, and a small basic toaster oven. I made tarts, cookies, and scones in there. I roasted small birds and vegetables, and used the toaster function to reheat without worry of burning, and to render lardons. It developed a very worn look by the end of the year I lived there, but I don't think it cost more than $25 at that point in time, and they can still be had for a minimal fee.

Japanese mandolin

This plastic tool makes fast, easy work of slicing and julienning. Just watch your fingers.

Weight scale

I like a thin digital one for better accuracy and for my New York City space restrictions, but any food scale will do. This will help you portion items that come in bulk such as pasta, cutting down on waste.

Small jar with lid

I learned this trick from my high school friend Philip Anderson and his food-writer mother, Susan. They would make vinaigrette in the jar and keep it in the fridge, ready at any time to be shaken and added to salads. I generally keep a basic mustard vinaigrette around in one of these—all of the ingredients are shelf stable, so it doesn't make sense to make just a little at a time. (See page 157.)

Pot of herbs or an Aero herb garden

Fresh herbs don't last very long, and it always drove me crazy when I had to buy a $5 bunch of thyme and would only use a smidgen of it before it turned into gray compost material. So I grow my own. If you're lucky enough to have a garden, certainly do it there, but you can grow some on a sunny windowsill in a pot in the wintertime as well. Or, if you live in a big city and don't have access to good light, an Aero herb garden is a good alternative. You can grow herbs hydroponically with their special light bulbs. I'd suggest growing thyme, tarragon, parsley, basil, chives, and cilantro.

Wine Vacu Vin

A hand pump and rubber wine stoppers can help wine keep for a few days. Once the wine is oxidized, you can still cook with it, but this helps slow the oxidization. Better yet, if you have unlimited funds, or are simply a wine geek, a Coravin does a much better job—but comes at a price.

Small Things

A mini pie mold—I like a 4 x ⅔–inch nonstick mold. You still need to spray it with oil spray or butter and flour it before using.

- A small baking dish—I have a 4 x 3 x 1½–inch ceramic one.
- A small sauté pan, 5–6 inches across.

Keeping your freezer organized can help you eliminate waste and save on your food budget, while being more eco-friendly. It can also help you decide what to eat if you're having one of those days. Here are a few pro tips.

FIFO! First In, First Out

Whether you have a bottom-drawer top-loading freezer, or a cabinet-style front loader, it's best to keep the oldest items at the top or in the front, putting the newest items to the end of the line at the back. While it is not imperative that you use ingredients exactly in order of age, as the shelf life of frozen goods is long, it does help to make sure nothing flounders forgotten in the icy depths, developing hoary ice burn beards—the jilted lovers of the frozen ingredient world. *And don't forget to label and date everything.*

Birds of a feather

Keep like items together. This will help you locate what you are looking for and save on time.

- Best to put cooked items on upper shelves and raw ingredients on the bottom; that way you don't risk chicken juice dripping onto something you might just reheat and eat.
- Group by ingredient type, lightest to darkest: vegetables to one side, followed by fish and shellfish, then chicken, duck, pork, beef, lamb, and game. Organize cooked foods in a similar fashion: stocks then soups, then braises, then meats . . .

Freeze in useable portions

· *Vacuum sealer:* If you buy a 1-pound package of bacon, for instance, separate it depending on how you think you'll use it (in increments of two or three slices, perhaps), then seal it that way, separated yet in the same bag. With vacuum sealer packaging, you can cut the bag open, take out what you need, then reseal the same package (and all the bacon will still be in the same place).

· *Ice cube trays:* If you make a bigger batch of sauce (such as chimichurri), use an ice cube tray to separate it into portions; once frozen, you can vacuum-seal it for better keeping, or simply place in a labeled and dated ziplock bag.

· *Cut before freezing:* If you find yourself with a large piece of meat or fish, weigh the whole to see how many portions you should be getting (5½–6 ounces per portion is standard), then cut before freezing so you don't have to defrost everything at once. Food generally doesn't like being refrozen—the texture is usually compromised if you have to do this. Cut bagels in half before freezing as well—then you can toast them from their frozen state.

Keep a log and cross items out as you use them

This is obviously just a suggestion, but the best chefs are insanely anal—we love charts. You can post this on the door of the freezer. Here's an example:

For instance, if you buy a package of bacon, you mark the first column "bacon." In the second box mark the purchase/freeze date, then mark in descending order how many portions you have in the following columns. As you use each portion, cross it off.

ITEM	DATE	PORTIONS					
VEGETABLES							
Frozen peas	12/5/15						
Edamame	11/30/15						
FISH AND SHELLFISH							
Frozen shrimp							
Alaskan sockeye	8/1/15	6	5	4	3	2	1
MEAT							
Chicken breasts	12/11/15	2	1				
Chicken legs and wings	12/11/15		1				
Skirt steak	11/3/15						
Bacon	12/22/15	6	5	4	3	2	1
Dumplings	11/8/15						
COOKED ITEMS							
STOCKS							
Chicken stock	12/11/15						
SAUCES							
Chimichurri	10/30/15	2	1				
MISCELLANEOUS							
Braised short rib	12/22/15						

How to defrost

The best way to defrost a piece of protein or a cooked item is to take it out the day before you plan to use it and allow it to slowly defrost overnight in the refrigerator. But if you need to quickly defrost something, put it in a bowl in its wrapper and allow a slow stream of cold water to flow over it. This should melt most single-portion items in twenty minutes or less.w

ACKNOWLEDGMENTS

I'd like to thank my editor, Lexy Bloom, and the team at Knopf for their hard work making this book a reality. Now that it's out, I can tell you that you were the *only ones* to believe in it as is. Thank you for being Solo! I'd also like to thank the illustrator, Julia Rothman, for her incredible artwork. Your drawings made this book so much more fun, and I'm especially thankful for not having to go through many tedious days of a photo shoot. Thanks also to my agent, Laura Nolan, for being the best and the brightest, for keeping me working, and for all of those delicious lunches! Thank you to David Ransome for the brainstorm of cookbook titles that included my last name, which ultimately led to this book. (Among his suggestions: *Lo Country Cooking, Lo and Slow Braising, Lo-Brow Cuisine: 101 American Greasy Spoon Recipes, Lo-Cal Cooking, LOcal Farm to Table*, and of course, *SoLo*). Thank you to my former staff at annisa. I probably stole some of your mise-en-place to test some of these recipes. And thank you to my better half, Mary Attea, whose patience, intelligence, keen palate, and boundless love make me feel less alone.

A NOTE ABOUT THE AUTHOR

Anita Lo is an acclaimed chef who worked at Bouley and Chanterelle before opening the Michelin-starred restaurant annisa in the heart of Manhattan's Greenwich Village in 2000, which she ran until it closed in 2017. *Food & Wine* named her one of the ten Best New Chefs in America, and *The Village Voice* proclaimed her Best New Restaurant Chef. She has appeared on *Top Chef Masters*, *Iron Chef America*, and *Chopped;* in 2015, she became the first female guest chef to cook for the White House. She lives in New York City and on Long Island.

A NOTE ON THE TYPE

This books was set in TheSerif, a typeface published in 1994 by the Dutch type designer Luc(as) de Groot (b. 1963). It is part of his Thesis superfamily, which also includes TheSans, TheMix, and TheAntiqua, some of which are available in monospaced and Arabic variants. TheSerif has sixteen different styles, offering a large range of possibilities. De Groot runs his type foundry LucasFonts in Berlin, his website stating, "His overall aim: to make the world a better place by designing typefaces that look pleasant and work well under any circumstances and in as many languages as possible."

. . . .

Composed by North Market Street Graphics,
Lancaster, Pennsylvania

Printed and bound by Toppan Leefung Printing, Ltd.,
Dongguan, China